SETTING THE STAGE

ARTICLES AND ESSAYS ABOUT THE STATE OF OUR WORLD TODAY

Edited and with Commentary by
Roger Pulvers

KENKYUSHA

SETTING THE STAGE
Articles and Essays about the State of Our World Today

Edited and with Commentary by Roger Pulvers
Copyright © 2005 by Roger Pulvers

Acknowledgements

"Towards a brave new world", from *The Stories of English* by David Crystal, published by The Overlook Press, copyright © 2004 by David Crystal / "Hidden power — Noam Chomsky on resurrecting the revolutionary spirit of America" by John Malkin, from *The Sun*, April 2005 issue, originally broadcast on Free Radio Santa Cruz, copyright © 2005 by John Malkin/ "A radical in the White House" by Bob Herbert, copyright © 2005 by The New York Times Co. Reprinted with permission / "The summit that couldn't save itself" by Naomi Klein, copyright © 2002 by Naomi Klein / "A new kind of challenge" by Fareed Zakaria, from *Newsweek*, May 9, 2005, copyright © 2005 by Newsweek, Inc. All rights reserved. Reprinted by permission / "Sick with worry" by Jerome Groopman, copyright © 2003 by Jerome Groopman / "Climate change: instant expert" by Fred Pearce, copyright © 2004 by Fred Pearce / "Great telescope race" by Nigel Henbest, copyright © 2004 by Nigel Henbest / "The Japanese language goes international", "Does language 'difficulty' speak of a sense beyond mere words?", "Thirty years on, have no lessons been learned from Vietnam?", "Memories are made of . . . history managed and manipulated?", "Where do the Japanese stand today?", "New horizons beckon as Train Man heads nowhere fast", "The stage is set for genuine change", "The art of Saito Makoto" by Roger Pulvers, copyright © 1993, 2000, 2005 by Roger Pulvers

Foreword

日本の学生が英語を学ぶ上でいちばん問題となるのは何か？ ぼくは日本ですでに 40 年近く日本人に英語を教えている。また、南は沖縄の八重山から北は北海道の札幌まで足を運んで、日本人の先生方に講演もたくさんしてきた。その結果、日本人の学生が英語を学ぶ上で一体何に悩んでいるのか、それがわかったのだ。彼らの悩みは単純だ。「どうすれば英語で自己表現できるか？」ということである。

多くの先生方は、そのためには「語彙を増やさなければならない」というだろう。文法やリスニングの大切さを説く先生方もいるだろう。もちろんそれらはすべて大切だ。

しかし、大事なことを忘れてはいけない。英語教育は、学習者一人ひとりの人間としての幅を——文化的に、社会的に、感情的に——広げるためになされるべきものだ。自分を表現するためには、言いたいことを持たなければならない。ぼくはこれを心に留めて、このまったく新しい大学テキストの編纂に取りかかった。

本テキスト *Setting the Stage — Articles and Essays about the State of Our World Today* にはテーマ別に合計 16 本の記事を収録した。どれも今日の英語圏で起こっていることを正確に伝えるものであると思う。国際的な雑誌 *Newsweek*, イギリスの新聞 *The Guardian* や *The Independent* や雑誌 *New Scientist*, アメリカの新聞 *New York Times* や雑誌 *New Yorker*, さらには日本の新聞 *The Japan Times*（*The Japan Times* でぼくは今年の 4 月から毎週日曜日掲載の連載コラム *Counterpoint* を担当している）などから記事を厳選し、収録した。注意深く選んだこれらの記事を読むことによって、日本の学生諸君は、日本語で書かれたものではなかなか得られない貴重な情報を手に入れることができると思う。学生諸君には、ぼくが厳選したこれらの記事を読むことで、新しい角度から物事を見られるようになり、書かれたニュースの背後にある事実を突き止められるようになってほしい、と心から願っている。このテキストは、今日の日本の学生諸君に最新の情報を与えるだろう。しかもその情報は、ただ新しいだけでなく、何年も古びることはないと思う。

重要なのは、日本人が英語で何か言いたいのであれば、日本と世界に対して揺るぎない視点や考え方を身につけなければならない、ということである。それさえ身につければ、自分自身の意見を持つことができる。自分自身の考えを英語で表現できれば、相手にも耳を傾けてもらえる！ 英語を話すのは、いくつかの英単語を正確に発音すればいい、というものでは決してない。ネイティヴスピーカーは、相手がいかに英語をうまく話すかより、自分に「何を話してくれるか」に関心があるのだ。

このテキストを編纂するにあたって、日本で出版されている英語のテキストに何冊も目を通した。

語注をつけているものもたくさんあったが、ほとんどは表面的な英語の意味しか載せていなかった。ぼくはこれまで日本人の学生諸君に長く英語を教えてきて、彼らの英語学習に一体何が必要か、よく理解しているつもりだ。彼らは生きた英語（living English）に触れなければならない。今日の日常会話で用いられる英語を理解しなければならない。

例えば、THE WORLD TODAY の "A new kind of challenge" に、". . . he talked about our agenda, not just his agenda." という表現が出てくる（55ページ、15–16行）。この agenda はどういう意味だろうか？

agenda を辞書で引けば、「予定表、計画表、（会議用の）議事日程、会議事項」といった語彙定義が出てくるが、これでは何のことかよくわからない。しかし、日常よく使われるような言い方を示しつつ説明してやれば、学生諸君はこの意味をしっかりつかめるはずだ。

例　Ishihara talks about peace, but he has a different agenda.（石原はよく「平和」を口にするが，実は別のことを企んでいる．）

例　My agenda is simply that I want to graduate. I'm not trying to curry favor with the teacher by giving him a present.（ぼくはただ卒業したいだけだ．先生に貢物をしてご機嫌を取るなんてことはしないさ．）

このように、agenda は日常会話では「これから考えること」の意味でよく使われる。

また、JAPAN の "Where do the Japanese stand today?" には、"Personal pride stemmed from how much you contributed to the whole without making undue demands on the common bounty." という表現が出てくる（68ページ、10–12行目）。この stem from という表現は、はたしてしっかり理解できているだろうか？

この stem は、「（...から）生じる、生じる、起こる、由来する」という意味であるが、次のような用例を示して説明すれば、すぐにわかってもらえると思う。

例　Jack's inability to speak Japanese stems from his total lack of interest in languages.（ジャックが日本語が全然しゃべれないのは，ことばというものにまったく興味がないからさ．）

このように辞書を引いても今ひとつ意味のつかみにくい語や表現については、スペースの許す限り、日常会話で使われる用例を示しながら説明した。（用例の前には、例 という印をつけてある。学生諸君は予習のさいには、本文だけでなく、語注もしっかり読んでほしい。）

こうした用例のほか、時事的な情報（これもやはり重要である）もかなり付けた結果、本テキストの語注は膨大なものになってしまった。しかし、ぼくは考えに考えてそれらの語に注を付けた。だから、学生諸君はこれらの注をしっかり読んで、今日のジャーナリズムの文章に使われる語や表現の背後にあるほんとうの意味を理解できるようになってほしい。

そして各記事の終わりには練習問題（リーディング8問、リスニング2問）も用意した。特にリーディング問題は TOEIC や TOEFL などの試験で出題される形式に近いものであるから、学生諸君はこれで試験前の腕試しをしていただきたい。

また本テキストの最後に、小説（fiction）も1本収録した。自己表現するには、小説を読むこと

も大事なのだ。（しかし、ここでは注は最小限にとどめて、問題も省略した。小説の読み方には答えがないし、読者に「このように読むべきだ」と強制することがあってはならない、とぼくは考えるからだ。）

　ぼくは教師として、作家として、自分の人生を日本に捧げてきた。

　今の日本の若い人たちが、愉快で、表現力豊富で、創造的人物となるのを、この目で確認できるのであれば、これほどうれしいことはない。ぼくが本テキスト Setting the Stage を編纂したのは、そういったことがあるからなのだ。

　本書のタイトル "Setting the Stage" は元々演劇などで使われる表現で、to set the stage は「...のための舞台装置を整える」、あるいは比喩的に「お膳立てをする」という意味で用いられる。そこから、「準備を万端にして、あとは実際に演じればいい」という意味でも使われるようになった。ここでも例を二つ挙げる。

例　Hiroshi set the stage for Carol by telling a few jokes and introducing her speech in such a positive way.
　　浩志はキャロルに話をしてもらうのに先立ち、いくつかジョークを飛ばし、大いに彼女をほめちぎった。

例　The stage is set for peace in South Asia, because now the Indians are talking to the Pakistanis.
　　インドがパキスタンとの対話を開始しているので、南アジアに平和が訪れつつある。

　ぼくの本を読んでくれる日本の若い読者たちが、このテキストで英語を勉強することで、いざ世界に飛び出せることを、心から願っている。(It is my fervent wish that this textbook will set the stage for my young Japanese readers to step out into the world.)

2005 年 10 月 17 日
ロジャー・パルバース（Roger Pulvers）

CONTENTS

Foreword iii

ON LANGUAGE 3

The Japanese language goes international
by **Roger Pulvers** 4

Does language "difficulty" speak of a sense beyond mere words?
by **Roger Pulvers** 11

Towards a brave new world
by **David Crystal** 18

AMERICA AND THE WORLD 25

A radical in the White House
by **Bob Herbert** 26

Hidden power
Noam Chomsky on resurrecting the revolutionary spirit of America
by **John Malkin** 33

Thirty years on, have no lessons been learned from Vietnam?
by **Roger Pulvers** 41

THE WORLD TODAY 47

The summit that couldn't save itself
by **Naomi Klein** 48

A new kind of challenge
by **Fareed Zakaria** 54

Memories are made of . . . history managed and manipulated?
by **Roger Pulvers** 61

JAPAN 67

Where do the Japanese stand today?
by **Roger Pulvers** 68

New horizons beckon as Train Man heads nowhere fast
by **Roger Pulvers** 75

The stage is set for genuine change
by **Roger Pulvers** 82

SCIENCE AND TECHNOLOGY 89

Sick with worry
by **Jerome Groopman** 90

Climate change: instant expert
by **Fred Pearce** 97

Great telescope race
by **Nigel Henbest** 103

FICTION 111

The art of Saito Makoto
by **Roger Pulvers** 112

SETTING THE STAGE

Articles and Essays about the State of Our World Today

ON LANGUAGE

The Japanese language goes international

Roger Pulvers

introduction

日本語は、英語と違って、日本の国の人たちだけが話すことばである。その点では、たとえばポーランド語、ペルシア語、ノルウェー語、ナヴァホ語と同じだ。しかし、今日では、南アジアや中国やオーストラリアやアメリカから来た人たちが日本語を話すのも、決して珍しいことではなくなった。ぼくは1967年に初めて日本の土を踏んだが、その頃日本語を話す外国人はほとんどいなかった。

1980年代にいわゆる「ガイジン・ブーム」が起こり、それで状況が大きく変わった。あの時代、ぼくもその一人であったが、多くの外国人がテレビに出て日本語を話した。中には方言まで話す外国人もいた。そうした外国人の多くは、ヨーロッパ系（European origin）だった。（ぼくはCaucasian［白色人種の］とか、white［白人の］という言い方はなるべくしたくない。）

世界に日本語を話す外国人が増えれば増えるほど、日本人はますます自分を自由に表現できるようになるだろう。ぼくはそう強く信じたい。

I went into a department store to buy a fountain pen, examined some of the pricey items under the counter glass and asked the young saleswoman, in Japanese, if I might see one of them.

She stood as if transfixed, staring into my face for a long moment.

"Sorry, no English," she said to me in English. [5]

"Yes, it's all right," I assured her. "I am speaking Japanese now. You see that black lacquered pen next to the red one? May I please have a look at it?"

Once again she could only stare at me, her eyes gradually filling with the trepidation of acute embarrassment.

"One minute please," she replied again in English. "I am sorry." [10]

She hastily retreated to the safety of a back room, from where shortly after a man in his late 50s in a gray suit, necktie askew, emerged. He approached me, smiling.

"May I help you, sir?" he asked in English. "What do you wish to see?"

As you may have guessed, this is not a recent occurrence. In fact, it happened in the late 1960s, when a non-Japanese who spoke the language was still a rarity. The felicitous flip side of this cute bias was that all you had to say was "boo" in Japanese and people would call you fluent.

The Japanese then entertained the common notion that Japanese is a fiendishly difficult language, "the most difficult language in the world bar none," as [5] one taxi driver who spoke no other language once told me, adding that even though nonnative speakers may think that they understand Japanese, their appreciation of its expressions' subtleties is, in reality, essentially shallow.

It must be admitted that Japanese is, like all languages, full of wondrous subtlety; and the form that this takes may be ensconced in the most delicate [10] variations of tone. The Japanese are wont, for one thing, to abbreviate a response, to encapsulate a variety of nuances in a single word or phrase. The most revered type of individual in this society would have to be the person of few words . . . very few words. I learned this the hard way myself many years ago. [15]

A friend had come to visit me in Kyoto, a Buddhist architect named Chuck. I had been living over a year by then in Japan and fancied myself quite the glib linguist. Chuck, on the other hand, knew only one word of Japanese. And it was with this one word that he totally devastated me.

I had taken him to a favorite eel restaurant in Gion. While one of the eel [20]

[(p.4)9]　**trepidation**　おののき, 恐怖; 不安, 心配 (anxiety); 動揺.
[2]　**felicitous**　（言葉・表現が）うまい, 適切な.
[2]　**flip side [the~]**　（レコードの）裏面, B面;（比喩的に）裏面, 反対の［もうひとつの］面.
[4–5]　**fiendishly**　悪魔のように; ひどく, 大変に.
[5]　**bar none**　例外なく, まったく, 断然.
[10]　**ensconce**　（...に）（快適に, 落ち着いて）座る, おさまる; 受身形で,「座っている, おさまっている」.
[11]　**wont**　（...）慣れて,（...するのを）常として. as he was wont to say は,「彼がよく言っていたように」.
[11]　**abbreviate**　（語・句を）（一部を残して）略して書く, 短縮する.
[12]　**encapsulate**　（...を）カプセルに入れる［包む］, 封じ込める; 簡約する, 要約する.
[13–14]　**person of few words**　無口な人, 口数が少ない人.
[17]　**glib**　口の達者な, 舌のよく回る, べらべらと口先だけの（言）語学者; 諸外国語に通じた人. a good [bad] linguist で,「語学の達者［不得手］な人」.
[19]　**devastate**　圧倒する, 打ちのめす.

ON LANGUAGE

dishes was being served, the chef himself came out to greet us; and I promptly launched into one of those awful displays of pretentiousness that we can only hope desert us as we grow older. I pointed out to Chuck and chef alike the differences between congers and lampreys, sharpnosed eels and broadnosed eels, all knowledge acquired from a treasured old book bought at a flea market, [5] "Dr. Tanaka's Japanese Fishes."

It was then that Chuck, balancing on his chopsticks a slice of eel so thin that it could slip into the space between his two front teeth, looked up from the tatami at the thoroughly bored chef and uttered his single word of Japanese. The chef's face immediately lit up and he turned to me, saying, "He speaks [10] much better Japanese than you!"

I tell you, if there had been an eel-hole in that tatami I would have taken a deep breath and slithered down it nose first. But I had to take my hat off to Chuck. He had taught me a priceless lesson about the Japanese language: Don't say in 50 words what you can say in one. [15]

Chuck's single word of Japanese, by the way, was "mezurashii," which in this context means "unusual or extraordinary." What Chuck said might be translated into English, "I have never had anything so wonderful as this before," thus proving the adage that "for every one Japanese word there are 10 English ones." [20]

I might add that Chuck's pronunciation was not a patch on his cunning grasp of Japanese lingual strategies. His "mezurashii" came out sounding something like the name of a famous Italian sports car: "Mazerat-chi."

More than 30 years have passed and the Japanese are now, thank goodness, pretty much used to nonnatives wrangling freely, if not always nicely, with [25]

---

[2]　**launch into ...**　...に身を乗り出す.
[2]　**pretentiousness**　もったいぶること, うぬぼれていること, 見えを張っていること.
[4]　**conger**　アナゴ.
[4]　**lamprey**　ヤツメウナギ.
[19]　**adage**　金言, 格言, 箴言(しん), ことわざ.
[21]　**be not a patch on ...**　...とは比べものにならない, ...よりはるかに劣っている. 例 The curries in restaurants in San Francisco are not a patch on those you get in Mumbai. (サンフランシスコのカレー屋は, ムンバイ[ボンベイ]にあるのとはまったく比べものにならないほどおいしくない.)
[25]　**wrangle**　口論する, 論争する, けんかする.

their language. It would probably be assumed by many salespeople in a department store today that pen-buying foreigners would speak enough Japanese to make their wishes known. But one stubborn myth, still cherished jealously by many Japanese people, is that some words are "too Japanese" for nonnative speakers to ever understand fully.

The wife of a Japanese author once told me that I would never grasp the true meaning of the word "nasake" . . . because "only we Japanese have nasake." You know, I never knew this. "Nasake" has lovely English equivalents such as "compassion," "empathy" and "kindliness," just to mention a few. She was making a comment less about the translation of her words than about the depth of her nationalism.

When Konishiki was not named a grand champion of sumo, some Japanese remarked that he lacked the proper amount of "hin," adding that this word was not translatable out of Japanese. I remember seeing references to this incident in the Western press in which the nonnative commentators seemed to accept this inane misconception. "Hin" means "refinement" or "dignity." The English word "breeding" also comes to mind. It wasn't a lack of "hin" on Konishiki's part that stood in the way of his promotion. It was a surfeit of bias on the part of the Japanese who made such a statement, hiding a disfigured prejudice behind the mask of pseudo-linguistic pretense.

We have all come a long way in the past few decades. The legend of the unique difficulty of the Japanese language and the bluster of its false mysticism are emitted, on the odd occasion, from the lips of misinformed nonlinguists and mistutored bigots. But I believe that the majority of Japanese people now see their own language as a vehicle for communication that is not destined for the exclusive use of one nationality, no longer a code for the secret transference of race-inspired messages.

The internationalization of the Japanese language that has taken place may

---

[18]　**surfeit**　過剰; 氾濫.
[22]　**bluster**　吹き荒れ; 大騒ぎ; どなりつけること, 怒号, おどし; 大げさ［得意げ］な話し（ぶり）.
[24]　**mistutored**　悪い教育を受けた.
[24]　**bigot**　偏狭頑迷な人, 頑固者.

ON LANGUAGE

actually be the most positive and freeing change experienced by the Japanese people over recent years. Chuck was right. One word, said at the right time, not only speaks volumes: It also begins the process of rewriting the book.

---

[3] **speak volumes**　多くを語る．

[3] **It also begins the process of rewriting the book.**　厳密に言えば，この主語の It は，前のセンテンスの one word である．したがって，「(時機を外さずに発言されたことばは，多くを語る以上のこともする．)そこから日本語に対する考え方が変化し始めるのだ」という意味になる．この the book は「(物事の)基準，規範」，そして to rewrite the book で「(物事の)基準や規範を完全に変える」という意味になる．　例 Koizumi is rewriting the book on Japanese politics.（小泉は日本の政治を抜本的に変えている．）

Questions

1. In the 1960s, the felicitous aspect of the bias against using Japanese with foreigners was that

(A) a few words of Japanese by foreigners caused the Japanese to label them fluent
(B) Japanese people never really considered foreigners able to speak their language
(C) even fluent foreigners didn't know how to say "boo" in Japanese
(D) there were a few foreigners who spoke Japanese better than Japanese spoke English

2. According to the author, the Japanese revere the type of person who

(A) remains silent in the presence of foreign people
(B) uses a wide variety of nuances to express a simple idea
(C) learns things "the hard way," that is, through experience
(D) says things briefly, without a lot of extra explanation

3. The author got all his knowledge about eels from

(A) a Japanese chef
(B) reading a book
(C) his Japanese wife
(D) Chuck

4. Which of the below characterizes Chuck's ability to speak Japanese?

(A) He's actually pretty fluent.
(B) He can speak it better than the author himself.
(C) He knows only one word.
(D) He can't speak very well but he can read some Japanese.

5. The author writes that his friend Chuck taught him a very precious thing: "Don't say in 50 words what you can say in one." What does this mean?

(A) It does not pay to be overly talkative in Japanese.
(B) Words in Japanese are more repetitive than they are in English.
(C) The Japanese language is not as expressive as English.
(D) It doesn't help to read books in learning Japanese.

ON LANGUAGE

6. Which of these statements below best describes the "stubborn myth" referred to in this article?

(A) Japanese jealously cherish their language and don't want foreigners using it.
(B) Some Japanese words cannot be understood by foreigners.
(C) If you want to make your wishes known in Japanese, you have to have good pronunciation.
(D) Many Japanese now assume that foreigners speak at least a little Japanese.

7. The word "inane" on page 7, line 16, is closest in meaning to

(A) terrible
(B) wrong
(C) active
(D) ridiculous

8. The author states on page 7, line 21, "We have all come a long way in the past few decades." What does he mean by this?

(A) Most Japanese people now accept that foreigners can understand and use Japanese.
(B) Japanese is a uniquely difficult language, but that doesn't stop foreigners from studying it now.
(C) Misinformed nonlinguists will never speak a foreign language, be it Japanese or English.
(D) People like Chuck make better speakers of Japanese than the author.

You will hear the entire text of "The Japanese language goes international." Immediately following the text, you will hear Questions 9 and 10.
Listen carefully to the text and questions, and write your answers in the space provided below.

9. _____

10. _____

Does language "difficulty" speak of a sense beyond mere words?

Roger Pulvers

introduction

2004年12月から2005年7月まで、ぼくは小泉純一郎首相の私的諮問機関「文化外交の推進に関する懇談会」のメンバーとして討議に参加することができた。首相官邸で会議を重ねながら、ぼくは世界中の若い人たちに日本語を教えることの大切さを強く主張した。

戦時中、日本はアジア諸国に力ずくで日本語を浸透させようとした。しかし、今こそ日本は、自分たちの日本語を、平和のメッセージとともに、世界中に伝えるべきである。そうした「和」の精神と争いを避けようとする姿勢こそ、日本文化と日本人の人との付き合い方をいちばんよく表現するものなのだから。

「文化外交の推進に関する懇談会」の最後の会合で、小泉首相と町村信孝外務大臣は、海外での日本語教育の重要性、さらには今言ったような要素をしっかり備えた普遍的な日本文化の種を広く散布する大切さを強調した。

日本はすでに独特の地位を築いているのであり、そこから武力を使わず、そしてイデオロギーや宗教も押し付けず、自分たちの文化を世界中に広めることができるのだ。

I have often been told by Japanese people that theirs is the most difficult language in the world. Virtually all the Japanese people who have said this to me, I might add, have spoken no other language than their own.

The most conspicuous instance of this came my way in the mid-1980s when, one rainy night, I took a cab home from the station at Seijo Gakuenmae in Tokyo. No sooner had I closed my umbrella and entered the cab than the driver peered at me in the rearview mirror and said, in Japanese: "You're not a Japanese are you." [5]

"No, I'm not," I replied.

"Oh. Japanese is the most difficult language to speak in the world, you know. Isn't it?" [10]

Well, for the 15-minute ride home I strove to persuade my driver that this, in fact, did not seem to be the case. I pointed out the fiendish difficulties of the languages that I had studied in my life, Russian and, particularly, Polish being much more complicated in grammar and pronunciation, at least for a native speaker of English, than Japanese. I finished my discourse as we rounded the corner by my house.

"I mean, Polish, for instance, has elaborate case endings for adjectives, and even has a special one for the nominative plural of male animate nouns!" [5]

Having listened attentively to my passionate, if pedantic, foray into the esoterica of comparative linguistics, the driver stopped the cab by my front gate, turned his head around to me and smiled broadly.

"Well, anyway," he said, "Japanese is still the most difficult language in the world!" [10]

Now, for a non-native speaker, acquiring the ability to read and write Japanese takes tremendous effort. But my driver and I were discussing the spoken language, the medium by which most Japanese explain themselves to their compatriots and the outside world.

Japanese, of the languages that I know, is actually the easiest spoken language to master. [15]

For one thing, the number of words used in daily life is small compared to, say, English. Nuances in English are added by expressing an emotion with the use of any number of different words, incorporating layer upon layer of subtle meaning by dipping into what is an enormous chest of verbal riches. In Japanese, subtleties are added with the use of a variety of endings. When you get to the end of a sentence you can vary the tone, register and emphasis of what you say by using one or more of a number of word and sentence endings. These endings are not hard to master. The result is that a non-native can be very expressive and articulate in Japanese without having to learn thousands of words — in the case of English, words that came from Anglo-Saxon, Latin and the many other languages that have enriched its vocabulary. [20]
[25]

[(p.11)4]　**conspicuous**　はっきり見える，目立った，著しい．
[6]　　　　**pedantic**　学者ぶった，もの知り顔の．
[6]　　　　**foray**　（日常活動と違った分野に）一時手を出すこと，ちょっとした介入．
[7]　　　　**esoterica**　秘事；秘義，奥義．
[25]　　　 **articulate**　発音［言語］の明晰な，歯切れのよい；思想を表現できる；ちゃんと［はっきり］ものが言える．

And, you can pause, mumble, leave out core elements of sentences, even punctuate dialogue with long silences and still speak excellent Japanese! The other languages that I am familiar with do not allow for the huge pregnant pauses and embarrassing ellipses that allow valuable thinking time for non-native beginners. What is considered an acceptable pause in Japanese, often giving the impression of profundity, would be taken for pure prevarication in English.

Verbs are generally the horror element of language learning. In English they are irregular, with auxiliary verbs and the conditional to make matters worse. Slavic languages have the perfective and the imperfective, not to mention so-called verbs of motion. (You need a different verb for "to go" depending on whether you are walking or riding in something.) Japanese verbs are a cinch. Just change the ending of the verb's stem to get everything from "I eat" to "I ate," "I didn't eat," "I wouldn't have eaten," "I didn't want to eat," "even if I didn't want to eat" and "Sorry but I went and ate it," which is tabechatta. Easy as pie.

Why did my taxi driver at Seijo Gakuenmae persist in perpetrating the myth of difficulty? Is it just a benign ignorance of the workings of language, or is there something else at work here?

Is his quaint obstinacy an indication of a wished-for ethnic "exclusivity"?

I believe that this irrational belief in the difficulty of their language bestows upon Japanese people, willy nilly, a false mystique, as if through their language they were able to harbor secrets to which the outside world could never

---

[3]　**pregnant**　（この場合は）意味深長な，示唆的な，含み［含蓄］のある．
[4]　**ellipses**　（語の）省略．ellipses (/ɪlípsiːz/) は複数形で，単数形は ellipsis (/-səs/).
[6]　**prevarication**　言い紛らすこと，言いのがれること，ごまかすこと．
[9]　**auxiliary verb**　助動詞．
[12]　**cinch**　容易なこと，朝飯前．
[15–16]　(**as**) **easy** [**simple**] **as pie**　とてもたやすく，いとも簡単で，お茶の子さいさいで，朝めし前で．
[17]　**perpetrate**　（悪事・過失などを）犯す，しでかす (commit).
[18]　**benign**　（人・行為など)恵み深い，親切な，優しい．
[20]　**quaint**　風変わりでおもしろい，古風で趣きのある；奇妙な (odd).
[20]　**obstinacy**　頑固，強情．
[21]　**bestow**　授ける，贈与する
[22]　**willy-nilly**　いやでもおうでも，いやおうなしに．本文のように willy nilly とハイフンがなく2語で書かれることもある．

ON LANGUAGE

be privy. This false mystique allows them to entertain a feeling of national sharing without having to prove it explicitly. "We all think and feel the same way," it tells them, "and we can express this in a way that is only open to Japanese. The fact that non-Japanese cannot decipher this is proof of our ethnic cohesion." If they admit that the Japanese language is no harder than any other, and maybe even easier in some ways, their self-styled aura of exclusivity loses much of its shine.

Over the years, a number of Japanese politicians have dropped what are essentially racist clangers, the most famous perhaps being Prime Minister Yasuhiro Nakasone's unseemly remark about the "low intellectual level" of certain American minorities. These politicians, speaking in Japanese of course, put their foot in their mouth and yet are taken aback when foreign journalists vividly describe the heel protruding from their lips. Do they really think that their language is a code that cannot be deciphered by non-Japanese?

In former times it may have served the Japanese national cause for this country's people to be seen as shuffling in a foggy aura of inscrutability. By striving to be "not understood" and holding their cards close to their chest, so to speak, they bolstered their position. "We Japanese have a depth that you cannot fathom, and this is the source of our power." But in our explain-yourself-or-pay-the-price era, where the very survival of a nation's culture may depend on its ability to express its people's aspirations in a clear and

---

- [2] **explicitly** 明示的に，明白に，公然と；（言葉に出して）はっきりと，明確に；露骨に．
- [4] **decipher** （暗号・なぞを）解読する．
- [5] **cohesion** 密着，粘着；結合(力)；つながり．
- [9] **clanger** 大失敗，へま；失言．
- [12] **put one's foot in one's mouth** 困った失敗をする；へまなことを言って困った立場に陥る．
- [12] **be taken aback** 不意を討たれる，めんくらう，ぎょっとする（= be taken back）．
- [13] **the heel protruding from their lips** 口から踵(かかと)が突き出している．前の行の put their foot in the mouth にかけて言っている．
- [16] **shuffle** 足を引きずって（のろのろ）歩く．
- [16] **foggy** 霧[もや]の立ちこめた；霧がかかってぼんやりした．
- [16] **aura** この場合は(独特な)雰囲気，気配．
- [16] **inscrutability** （神秘的で曖昧模糊として）測り知れない，不可解な，なぞめいた；肉眼で見通せない．
- [18] **bolster** （弱い自信・所説など）支持[後援]する，守る．

unequivocal manner, the myth of difficulty is no more than an artificial obstacle, a high wall that locks Japanese people in more than it deters the rest of the world from entering.

    It is time that Japanese people rejoiced in the fact that people around the world can and, despite Japanese provincial biases and nostalgic predilections, [5] will understand them.

---

[1]   **unequivocal**   あいまいでない，明白な，明確な；疑う余地のない，無条件の，決定的な．
[2]   **deter**   （おじけづかせて）（...［するの］を）やめさせる，思いとどまらせる．
[5]   **predilection**   先入的愛好，偏愛，ひいき．

ON LANGUAGE

Questions

1. What did the author try to persuade the taxi driver of on the 15-minute drive home?

   (A) that he had studied other languages in his life, including Russian and Polish
   (B) that even though he wasn't a Japanese, it didn't mean that he couldn't become a Japanese
   (C) that only native speakers can speak languages fluently
   (D) that the most difficult language to speak is by no means Japanese

2. According to the article, what languages does the author speak?

   (A) English and Japanese
   (B) English only
   (C) English, Polish and Russian
   (D) English, Japanese, Russian and Polish

3. Did the taxi driver understand the difficulty of languages like Russian after hearing the author's prodigious and zealous explanation?

   (A) No, he didn't understand it at all.
   (B) Yes, he understood it completely.
   (C) Yes and no. He seemed to understand it a little bit.
   (D) He understood it but pretended that he didn't.

4. The author has often been told by Japanese that Japanese is the most difficult language in the world. The Japanese who have told him this primarily

   (A) speak only Japanese
   (B) speak Japanese and only one foreign language
   (C) don't know their own language very well
   (D) have never met a foreigner before

5. According to the author, how are nuances achieved in English?

   (A) by expressing emotion openly, unlike in Japanese
   (B) by accessing the huge vocabulary of words in English
   (C) by avoiding subtleties and being frank and direct
   (D) by expressing the conclusion at the beginning of the sentence

6. The word "fathom" on page 14, line 19, is closest in meaning to

(A) notice
(B) appreciate
(C) understand
(D) dive

7. According to the author, why do some Japanese persist in saying that Japanese is so difficult?

(A) because they are not very good at learning other people's languages
(B) because it gives them a sense of unity, shutting out foreigners
(C) because it allows them to entertain foreigners better and share their culture with them
(D) because speaking may be fairly easy, but reading and writing Japanese is extremely difficult

8. According to the author, why is it now important for the Japanese to be understood?

(A) because if a nation is not understood these days, it's culture may not continue to exist in a healthy state
(B) because in the past the difficulty of the Japanese language bolstered the country's position
(C) because everything is so expensive now and the Japanese will lose out if they don't learn other languages
(D) because the Japanese language locks Japan out from the rest of the world

You will hear the entire text of "Does language 'difficulty' speak of a sense beyond mere words?" Immediately following the text, you will hear Questions 9 and 10.

Listen carefully to the text and questions, and write your answers in the space provided below.

9. _____

10. _____

Towards a brave new world

David Crystal

Introduction

英語について論じた本は、数百冊、いや、数千冊あるかもしれないが、デイヴィッド・クリスタルが書いた *The Stories of English* は、そのなかでも際立ってすぐれた1冊である。「英語の物語」といっても、物語は一つではない、ということをぼくらは認識しなければならない。そのようにいくつも複雑に絡み合った英語ということばの歴史を、クリスタルはわかりやすく解きほぐして説明してくれる。

実に多種多様な方言や表現形態を通じて、英語は話され、文章の形で残されてきたわけで、実際、歴史や環境が今日ぼくらが知るものと異なっていれば、そのなかのいかなる方言や表現形態が英語の主流になっていてもおかしくなかった、と本書 *The Stories of English* は教えてくれる。英語を話す/話した人たちは、多くの国に住んでいる/住んでいたわけで、英語はまさにそうした何億にもおよぶ人たちの物語なのだ。

クリスタルは、この文章のなかで、「英語は今や(二つ以上の標準形式を持つ)多角的な言語である」(English has now become a pluricentric language.) と説く。さらには、英語の中心部は、今や英語を母語としない人たちが担いつつある、とさえ指摘する。

英語の中心部がそのように移行しつつあろうがなかろうが、これだけは確かに言える。英語の物語は、ぼくらがみんな一緒になって、現在なお執筆中だ。

Regional dialects of English have fought back against the hegemony of, first, a single standard language, and then a dual standard, British and American. In most places, they exist in a range of nonstandard varieties. In some countries, though, there are already clear signs of further 'regional standards' emerging, such as Australian English and Indian English. This is not surprising. There is no reason why the same processes which governed the consolidation of a standard variety within Britain and America should not manifest themselves in Australia, India, South Africa, or wherever a country is sufficiently concerned about its linguistic identity to institutionalize its usage in the form of regional dictionaries, grammars, pronunciation guides, and style manuals. Ironically, prescriptive attitudes once again arise, in these circumstances. The debates surrounding a question of what is the 'correct' form of Australian or Indian English can be just as heated as anything seen in eighteenth-century

Towards a brave new world

Britain. But there is a difference. In a pluricentric world, there is no longer a notion of general ownership.

Linguistic pluricentrism reflects the fact that, in the twenty-first century, nobody can be said to 'own' English any more. Or rather, everyone who has opted to use it has come to have a part-ownership in it. That is what happens to a language when it achieves an international or global presence. It belongs to all who use it. And when people adopt a language they immediately adapt it, to make it suit their needs. English has now become a pluricentric language — one whose norms and functions vary globally and develop independently according to sets of forces that no longer reflect the influence of a single (British or American) point of origin. Even a native-speaking point of origin is becoming less relevant as time goes by. The centre of gravity of the English language is steadily shifting from the native speaker to the non-native speaker. People who use English as a second or foreign language are now very much in the majority, with three non-native speakers in the world for every one native-speaker.

The literary implications are profound. Most English literature hitherto has come from people who speak English as a first or second language — that is, they learned their English in a country where the language had some kind of special status arising out of its colonial history. Commonwealth literature was one of the consequences of this situation. It remains to be seen what contribution will one day be made by those who have learned English as a foreign language — that is, from countries where English has had no colonial history but where fluent levels of competence are increasingly routine, such as Sweden, the Netherlands, and Denmark. Writing in English from such countries is currently always in Standard (British or American) English, but it will not always be that way. One day we will surely be reading Swedish English novels — that is, novels written by people who have Swedish as a mother

---

[(p.18)1]　**hegemony**　主導権, 覇権, ヘゲモニー.
[1]　　**pluricentric**　(言語が)二つ以上の標準形式をもつ, 標準形式併存の. たとえばイギリス英語とアメリカ英語という主要な標準形式をもつ英語を指して使われる. cf. a pluricentric language/a pluricentric view of English.
[17]　**hitherto**　今まで(は), 従来; 今までのところは(まだ).

tongue but who choose to write in a Swedish-coloured variety of English, analogous to Commonwealth literature today.

The concept of English as a pluricentric language has worried some people. It scared some of the British when the centre of linguistic gravity seemed to move to the United States. They listened to the words of the American writer Brander Matthews in 1900 with considerable trepidation:

> What will happen to the English language in England when England awakes to the fact that the centre of the English-speaking race is no longer within the borders of that little island? . . . Will the British frankly accept the inevitable . . . Will they follow the lead of the Americans when we shall have the leadership of the language, as the Americans followed their lead when they had it?

There was a flurry of British reaction. The Society for Pure English was founded by poet laureate Robert Bridges in 1913. Pamphlets were produced. The BBC stressed the importance of British English.

American English would in due course be put in its place just as much as the Americans thought British English had been. For even the United States — with some 230 million English speakers in the year 2000 — must now be seen as using a minority dialect of World English, with its total of over 1,500 million speakers of English as a first, second, or foreign language. Or rather, we see a set of minority dialects, for as the ethnic mix within the United States has grown, so has the range of regional and ethnic varieties of American English, and these are steadily broadening their presence in creative and functional domains such as the press, advertising, and broadcasting. And although the influence of American English on other countries remains far greater worldwide than that of any other kind of English, it has not prevented the progress or

---

[2]　**analogous**　（...に）類似して，相似で [to, with].
[6]　**trepidation**　おののき, 恐怖; 不安, 心配; 動揺.
[15]　**flurry**　（突然の）混乱, 動乱.
[16]　**poet laureate**　（英国の）桂冠(けいかん)詩人(国王任命の王室付き詩人). (the poet laureate, Poet Laureate とも書く. 複数形は poets laureate となる.)

fresh emergence of local varieties. The numbers are sometimes extremely significant: there are probably more English speakers in India today than in the whole of America and Britain combined. But even in places where the numbers are small, such as Singapore, the literary output displays an impressive vitality.

It is important to emphasize that Standard English, as manifested in its two main varieties, is not threatened by all these regional developments. That could hardly be, given that the vast majority of the world's printed English output is in either the British or American standard, or in a standard heavily influenced by one or the other (as in the case of Australia and Canada). Nor should we underestimate the common core of linguistic identity which unites them. Every few decades someone predicts that British and American English are one day going to become mutually unintelligible, but there is very little sign of this happening as far as the written language is concerned. When we add up all the differences between these two varieties — all the points of contrast in spelling, grammar, and vocabulary — we are talking about a very small part of the language as a whole. That, of course, is why we usually find the term 'Standard English' used without any regional qualification. We sense the common core.

But there is a second reason why the burgeoning of nonstandard varieties is no threat to the standard. Their function is different. Nonstandard varieties exist in order to express local identities, at a regional level. A standard variety exists to foster intelligibility, at a supra-regional level. In a world where there is an increasing need for international communication the role of a Standard English, whether in its British or American incarnation, remains secure. We need both kinds of variety, nonstandard and standard, if we are to participate fully in a local as well as an international world.

---

[1] **emergence** 出現; 発生.
[11] **underestimate** 実際より小さく[少なく]見積もる, 過小評価する, みくびる.
[19] **burgeon** 急に出現[発展]する; 芽ぐむ, もえ出る. 例 Tourism is a burgeoning industry in Yaeyama.（八重山では観光業が急速に伸びている．）
[22] **supra-** 上の, 上に.
[24] **incarnation**（観念・性質などの）権化, 化身;（人・事物の変化・転変における）一時期（の姿, 形）; 肉体を与えること, 人間化; 具体化, 実現.

ON LANGUAGE

Questions

1. By 'regional standards' on page 18, line 4, the author means

(A) standard usages of English forming in locations other than Britain and the U.S.
(B) people in Australia and India, for example, speaking standard English as fluently as people in Britain and the U.S.
(C) that grammar and pronunciation in Australian and Indian English, for example, are every bit as good as in Britain and the U.S.
(D) that, ironically, people in Australia and India, for example, are just not as correct in English usage as people in Britain and the U.S.

2. Commonwealth literature refers to

(A) literature written by nonnative speakers of English
(B) literature written in former British colonies
(C) literature written in countries where English had no colonial history
(D) literature written in countries like the Netherlands and Denmark where people are very competent in English

3. How would you characterize the English of people in countries like Sweden, the Netherlands and Denmark?

(A) Most people in such countries cannot speak English at all.
(B) Most people in such countries have a poor command of English.
(C) Most people in such countries can speak English but not read or write it.
(D) Most people in such countries are quite proficient in English.

4. When the British listened to the words of the American writer Brander Mathews in 1900, they were

(A) really glad to hear them
(B) bewildered or confused
(C) filled with admiration for the American writer
(D) sorry to hear them

5. The influence of American English has

(A) meant that most people in the world speak English with an American accent
(B) changed British ideas about accent and pronunciation
(C) not been able to stop new dialects of English from gaining ground
(D) caused people in countries such as Singapore to write books in English

6. According to the article, which country has the largest number of English speakers?

(A) India
(B) the United States
(C) Great Britain
(D) China

7. The word "burgeoning" on page 21, line 19, is closest in meaning to

(A) creating
(B) beginning
(C) budding
(D) appearing

8. The author states that the function of standard and nonstandard English is different. Why?

(A) People speaking nonstandard English can still communicate on a supra-national level.
(B) Nonstandard English is used by people as a voice for their own ethnic and national purposes.
(C) Standard English is used in the press, advertising and broadcasting.
(D) Nonstandard English is no threat to standard English.

You will hear the entire text of "Towards a brave new world." Immediately following the text, you will hear Questions 9 and 10.
Listen carefully to the text and questions, and write your answers in the space provided below.

9. _____

10. _____

AMERICA AND THE WORLD

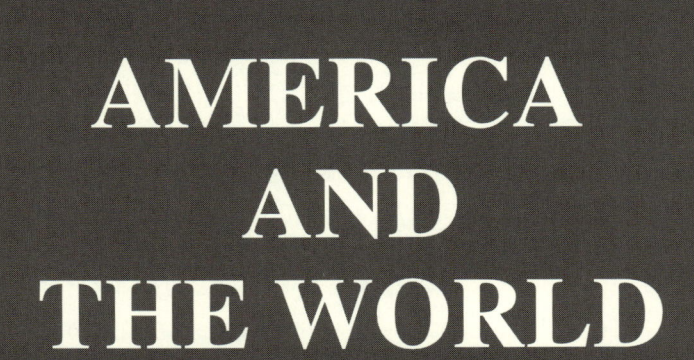

A radical in the White House

Bob Herbert

introduction

FDR の通称で知られる Franklin Delano Roosevelt（1882–1945）は、アメリカ第 32 代大統領である。三期以上に渡って大統領を務めたのは、彼だけだ。（FDR は 1933 年から 1945 年までアメリカの最高職に就いていた。）FDR は 4 期目の 1945 年の 4 月に、脳溢血で死去した。

民主党の大統領であった FDR は、政府は国民の生活を良くする義務がある、と強く信じていた。彼が真のリベラリズムを唱えたのは、妻エレノア（Eleanor）の影響が大きいと思う。エレノアは若い頃、ニューヨーク市のスラム街でソーシャルワークに携わっていた。（エレノアは、裕福な家庭に生まれた FDR に、借家暮らしをする人たちの生活ぶりを一度見せてまわったことがある。FDR はこれによってニューヨーク市には貧しい暮らしをする人たちもいることを知ったのだ。）

FDR は大統領としてアメリカ国民を導きながら、世界恐慌と第二次大戦をくぐり抜けた。しかし、第二次大戦の終結をその目で確認することはなかった。FDR は「ニューディール政策」を提唱した偉大なる改革者として語られることが多いが、彼はアメリカ国民に対して、政府は富裕階級の道具ではなく、国民すべてが求めることに応えるために存在するのだ、と明言した。

筆者ボブ・ハーバートは本文中で FDR が演説で述べた「2 番目の権利章典」（FDR's second Bill of Rights）」について紹介しているが、まさにそのもとになっているのが、この賞賛すべき考え方なのである。ハーバートは、それを示すことによって、FDR の理想と、そしてジョージ・W・ブッシュの利己的な政策を、対比している。

ぼくは、FDR が残したいちばん偉大なることばは——彼はアメリカが忘れてしまったと思えるようなことばをいくつか残している——、1945 年 1 月 20 日の 4 期目の大統領就任演説で述べたものだと思う。それは第二次大戦でアメリカが学んだことに結びつけた演説だった。

「われわれは一人では生きられないことを学んだ。一人では平和に生きられないことを学んだ。すなわち、われわれが幸福でいられるかどうかは、遠く離れた国々の人たちが幸福でいられるかどうかにかかっているのだ、ということを学んだ」（We have learned that we cannot live alone, at peace; that our own well-being is dependent on the well-being of other nations far away.）

「われわれは世界市民であることを学んだ。人間社会の一員であることを学んだ」（We have learned to be citizens of the world, members of the human community.）

「エマソンが言ったように、われわれは単純なことを学んだ。すなわち、『友だちを持つただ一つの方法は、自ら進んで誰かの友だちになることである』」（We have learned the simple truth, as Emerson said, that "The only way to have a friend is to be one"）

A radical in the White House

Last week — April 12, to be exact — was the 60th anniversary of the death of Franklin Delano Roosevelt. "I have a terrific headache," he said, before collapsing at the Little White House in Warm Springs, Ga. He died of a massive cerebral hemorrhage on the 83rd day of his fourth term as president. His hold on the nation was such that most Americans, stunned by the announcement of his death that spring afternoon, reacted as though they had lost a close relative. [5]

That more wasn't made of this anniversary is not just a matter of time; it's a measure of the distance the U.S. has traveled from the egalitarian ideals championed by F.D.R. His goal was "to make a country in which no one is left out." [10] That kind of thinking has long since been consigned to the political dumpster. We're now in the age of Bush, Cheney and DeLay, small men committed to the

---

[4]　**massive**　大きくて重い[堅い]；どっしりした；（頭・体格・容貌などが）大きい，がっちりした．この場合は，「大規模な，大きな，大量の；重症の」．

[4]　**cerebral hemorrhage**　脳出血，脳溢血（いっ）．

[5]　**stun**　この場合は，「(人に)（反応できないほどの）驚き[ショック]を与える，呆然自失に陥らせる」．

[8]　**That more wasn't made of this anniversary ...**　これはちょっとむずかしいかもしれない．まず，最初の That は次のような使われ方をする．例 That Kurosawa is Japan's best film director is known by everyone.（黒澤が日本最高の映画監督であるのは，誰もが知っていることだ[衆目の一致するところだ]．）次に，more wasn't made of this anniversary だが，ここでは make ... of ...（...を...にする）という言い方を考えてみなければならない．これは，例えば make a teacher of my daughter（娘を教師にする）というように用いられる．ここでは made more of this anniversary が受身形になって，more wasn't made of this anniversary となっている．more となっているのは，著者の頭のなかにおそらくは「9・11 の 1 周年のセレモニーはにぎやかに行なわれたが，FDR の没後 60 周年はそれほど話題にならなかった」ということがあるからだと思う．したがって，この文章は，「FDR の没後 60 周年はそれほど話題にならなかったが，それは単にそれから長い時間が経ってしまったからではない[単なる時間だけの問題ではない]」といった意味になる．make more of ... に似た表現に，make much of ...（...を重んじる，大事にする）があるので，あわせて覚えておこう．例 Don't make so much of it. It's no big deal.（くよくよしないで，大したことないよ．）

[9]　**egalitarian**　平等主義．発音にも注意（/ɪgælətéəriən/）．

[11]　**consign**　引き渡す；ゆだねる，託する，任せる．

[11]　**dumpster**　大型のごみ収集容器．（米国の金属製のごみ収集箱 Dumpster から．）

[12]　**Cheney, Dick**（1941–）　ディック・チェイニー．米国の政治家．78 年に連邦下院議員に初当選（共和党）し，George Bush（父）政権では国防長官を務めた．そして George W. Bush 大統領が 2001 年に大統領になると，副大統領に就任．2005 年にブッシュ再選後も引き続き副大統領．

concentration of big bucks in the hands of the fortunate few.

To get a sense of just how radical Roosevelt was (compared with the politics of today), consider the State of the Union address he delivered from the White House on Jan. 11, 1944. He was already in declining health and, suffering from a cold, he gave the speech over the radio in the form of a fireside chat.

After talking about the war, which was still being fought on two fronts, the president offered what should have been recognized immediately for what it was, nothing less than a blueprint for the future of the United States. It was the clearest statement I've ever seen of the kind of nation the U.S. could have become in the years between the end of World War II and now. Roosevelt referred to his proposals in that speech as "a second Bill of Rights under which a new basis of security and prosperity can be established for all regardless of station, race or creed."

Among these rights, he said, are:

"The right to a useful and remunerative job in the industries or shops or farms or mines of the nation.

"The right to earn enough to provide adequate food and clothing and recreation.

"The right of every farmer to raise and sell his products at a return which will give him and his family a decent living.

"The right of every businessman, large and small, to trade in an atmosphere of freedom from unfair competition and domination by monopolies at home or abroad.

"The right of every family to a decent home.

"The right to adequate medical care and the opportunity to achieve and enjoy good health.

"The right to adequate protection from the economic fears of old age, sickness, accident and unemployment.

[(p.27)12] **DeLay, Tom** (1947–) トム・ディレイ．1984年から現在までテキサス州22区選出の連邦下院議員．2005年，Ronny Earle テキサス州検事長に企業献金の不当流用を指摘され，全米で大きな問題になった．

[5] **a fireside chat** 炉辺談話，おしゃべり．(FDR が発表の形式として採った)炉辺談話から．

[15] **remunerative** 利益[収益]のある，報酬のある；引き合う，有利な．

"The right to a good education."

I mentioned this a few days ago to an acquaintance who is 30 years old. She said, "Wow, I can't believe a president would say that."

Roosevelt's vision gave conservatives in both parties apoplexy in 1944 and it would still drive them crazy today. But the truth is that during the 1950s and '60s the nation made substantial progress toward his wonderfully admirable goals, before the momentum of liberal politics slowed with the war in Vietnam and the election in 1968 of Richard Nixon.

It wouldn't be long before Ronald Reagan was, as the historian Robert Dallek put it, attacking Medicare as "the advance wave of socialism" and Dick Cheney, from a seat in Congress, was giving the thumbs down to Head Start. Mr. Cheney says he has since seen the light on Head Start. But his real idea of a head start is to throw government money at people who already have more cash than they know what to do with. He's one of the leaders of the G.O.P. gang (the members should all wear masks) that has executed a wholesale transfer of wealth via tax cuts from working people to the very rich.

Roosevelt was far from a perfect president, but he gave hope and a sense of the possible to a nation in dire need. And he famously warned against giving in to fear.

The nation is now in the hands of leaders who are experts at exploiting fear,

---

[4]   **apoplexy**　卒中.
[7]   **momentum**　はずみ，勢い，推進力.
[10] **Medicare**　（アメリカの）メディケア．65歳以上を対象とした医療保障（制度）．
[11] **Head Start**（= **Project Head Start**）　ヘッドスタート；ヘッドスタート計画．1964年米連邦政府が Economic Opportunity Act（経済機会法）によって始めた教育事業．「文化的に恵まれない」就学前の子供たちに教育・医療などのサービスを提供し，父母や地域にもこうした事業に参加させようとするもの．好評だったため，1967年幼稚園児のための Follow Through 計画が追加された.
[12] **Mr. Cheney says he has since seen the light ...**　since の位置がおかしいと思う人もいるかもしれないが，これは正しい．「それから；...以来」の意味で，次のように使われる．例 I have since changed my mind.（わたしはそのあと［そのことがあってから］考え直した．）例 I have since come to love her.（ぼくはあれから彼女のことが好きになった．）
[14] **G.O.P.**（= **the Grand Old Party: GOP**）　共和党（the Republican Party）のこと．1880年からその愛称で呼ばれる．
[18] **dire**　ここでは，「（必要・危険など）差し迫った」．

AMERICA AND THE WORLD

and indifferent to the needs and hopes, even the suffering, of ordinary people.

"The test of our progress," said Roosevelt, "is not whether we add more to the abundance of those who have much; it is whether we provide enough for those who have too little."

Sixty years after his death we should be raising a toast to F.D.R. and his [5] progressive ideas. And we should take that opportunity to ask: How in the world did we allow ourselves to get from there to here?

---

[5] **raise a toast** （...のために）祝杯をあげる，（...に）乾杯する．

A radical in the White House

Questions

1. What does the author mean by "his hold on the nation" on page 27, line 5?

(A) The American people were shocked to learn how he died.
(B) The American people were stunned that the anniversary wasn't celebrated as it should be.
(C) The American people felt very loyal and close to F.D.R.
(D) The American people felt that the country was in the grip of egalitarian ideals.

2. According to the article, the 60th anniversary of the death of FDR was

(A) celebrated with much enthusiasm
(B) not widely discussed by American citizens
(C) hailed by Bush, Cheney and DeLay
(D) a cause for much anger in America

3. The word "egalitarian" on page 27, line 9, is closest in meaning to

(A) the principle of equality
(B) the principle of inequality
(C) the principle of discrimination
(D) the principle of capitalism

4. The author calls Roosevelt "radical" on page 28, line 2. Why?

(A) because no other president had served four terms before
(B) because the nation had not become the kind of nation that he envisaged
(C) because of the ideas stated in a "fireside chat"
(D) because he failed in his policies

5. Which is NOT a right referred to by FDR in his "Second Bill of Rights" on page 28, line 11?

(A) The right of every family to a decent home
(B) The right to a good education
(C) The right to adequate medical care
(D) The right of free competition

AMERICA AND THE WORLD

6. Why was the author's 30-year-old acquaintance so surprised by what F.D.R. said?

(A) because his ideas seemed progressive even by today's standards
(B) because presidents don't usually talk about big ideas
(C) because the nation had made substantial progress toward these goals in the 1950s and '60s
(D) because the Bill of Rights in the constitution already included many of these policies

7. Which of the following politicians objected to Head Start as a Congressman?

(A) Ronald Reagan
(B) Robert Dellek
(C) Dick Cheney
(D) George W. Bush

8. What does the author mean by "the test of progress" on page 30, line 2?

(A) that if we add to the abundance of everyone, even those who have little will benefit
(B) that progress is judged by how few poor people there are, not by how many rich people there are
(C) that progressive ideas of Roosevelt's time are largely invalid today
(D) that we should always ask the question: What can we do to give opportunity to young and old?

You will hear the entire text of "A radical in the White House." Immediately following the text, you will hear Questions 9 and 10.
Listen carefully to the text and questions, and write your answers in the space provided below.

9. _____

10. _____

Hidden power
Noam Chomsky on resurrecting the revolutionary spirit of America

John Malkin

introduction

1964 年、ぼくはマサチューセッツ州ケンブリッジのハーバード大学大学院で学んでいたが、ハーバードからそれほど遠くない MIT では、言語学者のノーム・チョムスキー教授が教鞭を執っていた。アメリカがベトナムで戦争を起こしたことによって、チョムスキー教授はアメリカの帝国主義を厳しく批判するようになったのだと思う。今日、ノーム・チョムスキーは、近代言語学の父としてのみならず、政治思想家としても知られている。

　この 2004 年 11 月 19 日に行なわれた John Malkin によるインタビューにおいて、チョムスキーは民主主義に対する揺るぎない信念をさらに固めながら、「...国民は参加し、どうするか決めなければならない...」(...the people must participate and make decisions...) と述べている。

　母国アメリカの指導者たちが作り上げた神話のまさに根本部分を、彼らがそのような判断を下した密かな動機を、チョムスキーは常に問いただす。ノーム・チョムスキーは、ぼくと同年代の人たちだけでなく、若い世代の人たちのヒーローの一人だ。彼のような人が日本にも出てきてくれたらいいのだが...

This interview took place on November 19, 2004 at the Massachusetts Institute of Technology, in Cambridge. The interviewer is John Malkin.

Malkin: Many people in this country became politically active, some of them for the first time, during this year's presidential campaign. A lot of them [5] are now expressing despair and disappointment about the election results. What are your thoughts about the recent election?

Chomsky: Well, such despair is common, but it is the result of a misunderstanding. For one thing, elections tell us virtually nothing about the country. George W. Bush got about 31 percent of the electorate. John Kerry got about [10] 29 percent. That leaves 40 percent of Americans who didn't vote. The voting patterns were almost the same as in 2000: same "red" states, same "blue" states. There was only a slight shift that tipped the election in Bush's favor. Apparently the wealthier part of the population — which tends to vote more in line with its class interests — came out in somewhat greater numbers this time. If the voting patterns had shifted slightly in the opposite direction and Kerry were in the White House, it would also tell us nothing about the country. [5]

Right before the election there were extensive studies released about voters' attitudes and intent. It turns out that only about 10 percent of them were voting for what the studies' designers called "agenda, policies, programs, and ideas." The rest were voting for imagery.

U.S. elections are run by marketing professionals, the same people who sell [10] toothpaste and cars. They don't believe in actual free markets or the nonsense taught in school about informed consumer choice. If they did, GM ads would say, "Here are the models we are putting out next year. Here are their characteristics." But they don't do that, because their model is the same as the next company's model. So what they do is show you an actress or a football player [15] or a car going up a sheer cliff. They try to create an image that will trick you into buying their product.

These marketers also construct imagery to try to influence elections. They train Bush to project a certain image: An average guy just like you. A guy you'd like to meet in a bar. Someone who has your interests at heart, who'll [20] protect you from danger. Kerry is trained to project a different image: someone who cares about the economy and about people's health, a war hero, and so on. Most people vote for an image, but the image typically has almost no resemblance to reality. People tend to vote for the candidate they believe shares their values. They are almost always wrong. Working-class Bush voters believed [25] that Bush supported their interests, when the Republican Party platform was mostly about redirecting wealth to the top.

[(p.33)10]　**electorate**　選挙人.
[(p.33)12]　**"red" states**　共和党支持の州.
[(p.33)12–1]　**"blue" states**　民主党支持の州.
[8]　**agenda**　協議事項，議題．55ページの注も参照のこと．
[11]　**toothpaste**　練り歯磨き.
[13–14]　**characteristic**　特質，特色，特徴，特性.
[26]　**platform**　この場合は，「政綱，綱領」.

Hidden power

If you ask people why they don't vote based on issues, they'll say, "I don't know where the candidates stand on the issues." Which is the truth. The election is designed to keep you from understanding the candidates' positions on the issues. To figure out, say, what their healthcare proposals are would require a major research project. You aren't supposed to know. The advertising industry wants you to focus on what they call "qualities." And when you do discover the candidates' positions on the issues, you understand why.

Right before the election, two of the best public-opinion organizations in the world came out with major studies of popular attitudes and beliefs. The results are so far to the left of either political party that the press can't even report it. Huge majorities think that their tax dollars ought to go first for healthcare, education, and Social Security — not the military. An overwhelming majority oppose the use of military force unless we are under attack or under imminent threat of attack. A majority of Americans are in favor of signing the Kyoto Protocol on Climate Change and subjecting the U.S. to the International Criminal Court. The large majority think that the UN, not the United States, ought to take the lead on international crises. In fact, the majority even support giving up the U.S.'s veto power in the UN Security Council, so that the U.S. will have to go along with the opinions of the majority. I could go on, but these positions are so far off the left end of the political spectrum that you can understand why

---

[10] **left** （政治的・思想的に）左派の，革新的な．

[14–15] **Kyoto Protocol on Climate Change** 正式名称は，気候変動に関する国際連合枠組条約の京都議定書（Kyoto Protocol to the United Nations Framework Convention on Climate Change）．気候変動枠組条約に基づき，1997年に京都市の国立京都国際会館で開かれた地球温暖化防止京都会議（第3回気候変動枠組条約締約国会議，COP3）で議決した議定書．地球温暖化の原因と見られる大気中の温室効果ガス（二酸化炭素，メタン，亜酸化窒素など）について，先進国における削減率を定め，共同で約束期間内に目標を達成するというもの．2008年〜2012年の間に，日本マイナス6%，アメリカマイナス7%，EUマイナス8%といった削減率を設定している．発展途上国の自発的参加が見送られ，世界最大の二酸化炭素発生国であるアメリカ合衆国が受け入れを拒否，ロシア連邦も受け入れの判断を見送っていたため，議定書の発効が危ぶまれていた．2004年にロシアが批准したため発効が確定した．

[15] **subject** （...を）（...に）服従させる，従わせる，従属させる．

[15–16] **the International Criminal Court** 国際刑事裁判所．

[18] **veto power**（= veto） 国連の安全保障理事会で常任理事国に与えられている拒否権．

[18] **the UN Security Council** 国連安全保障理事会．

the advertising industry has to keep issues out of the election and focus on imagery.

The way to overcome this situation is to create real political parties. To have real political parties, the people must participate and make decisions, not just come together once every four years to pull a lever. That is not politics. It is the opposite of politics. If you have mass popular organizations that are functioning all the time — at local, regional, and international levels — then you have at least the basis for a democracy. Such organizations existed here in the past. The unions were one example.

Meaningless formal elections are indeed what the elite want us to have in this country. It goes back to the Constitutional Convention of 1787, where James Madison laid it out: the power has to be in the hands of the wealthy of the nation, he said, people who understand the needs of property owners and recognize that the first priority of government is to protect the wealthy minority from the unwashed majority. To do this, the elite must fragment the majority in some fashion. We have had two-hundred-plus years of struggle about this because the people don't accept it, and they have gained many rights as a result of that struggle. In fact, we have a legacy of freedom that is in many ways unique. But it wasn't granted from above. It was won from below. And the battle continues.

The wealthy and privileged are always fighting a bitter, unremitting class war. They never stop for a minute. If one tactic doesn't work, they shift to another. And if the general population lets itself become pessimistic and gives up — which is what the elite want — then the upper class will be even more free to do whatever is in its own best interest.

Malkin: It seems that, to the rest of the world, the propaganda that manipulates U.S. public opinion has been transparent for some time. Do you think the deceit is becoming more clear to people within the United States? Given the revelation that Iraq did not have weapons of mass destruction, the hiring of

---

[12]　**Madison, James**（1751–1836）ジェームズ・マディソン．米国の第4代大統領．
[15]　**fragment**　ばらばらにする[なる]，分解[分断]する．
[28]　**deceit**　欺くこと，虚偽，欺瞞，詐欺；欺くための術策，欺術，ごまかし，うそ，ペテン．

Halliburton to clean up after the war, the Abu Ghraib torture scandal, and this week's reports of a U.S. soldier executing an unarmed Iraqi, do you think people in the United States are waking up to the deception?

Chomsky: I don't want to be impolite, but the list you have just given is itself a type of sophisticated propaganda. Take the marine who killed an unarmed man in a Fallujah mosque. Compared with everything else that's going on in Fallujah, is that an atrocity? It isn't even a minor footnote. The atrocity is what you read on the front page of the *New York Times*, where you'll see a picture of Iraqi patients and doctors lying on the floor, manacled, and U.S. soldiers standing guard over them. The front-page story tells us proudly that American soldiers broke into Fallujah General Hospital, forced patients out of their beds, and made them lie on the floor in handcuffs. That is a war crime. The Geneva Conventions, which are the foundation of modern humanitarian laws, say that hospitals must be protected at all times, by all sides, in a war.

But of course the *Times* doesn't describe that hospital invasion as a war crime. The *Times* says it was an achievement, because Fallujah General Hospital was a propaganda center for the insurgents. Why? Because it was producing inflated casualty reports. How do we know that the reports were inflated? Because our leader told us so, and if our leader says something, it is automati-

---

[1]　**Halliburton (～ Co.)**　ハリバートン（社）米国の油田開発・サービス会社．産業用海洋構造物建設，特殊産業装置の製造，保険にも進出．1924年設立，60年から現社名．本社はテキサス州ヒューストン．ハリバートン社は米政府からイラク復興関連でガソリンなどの燃料輸入や米軍基地への給食提供，軍需補給業務など多額の発注を受けた．しかし，契約額が高すぎるため，水増し請求した疑いが指摘され，国防総省が調査を開始．3月にはガソリン燃料輸入に関するハリバートン社との契約を撤回し，他社と新契約を結んでいる．チェイニー米副大統領がハリバートン社の最高経営責任者（CEO）を務めていたこともあり，副大統領と同社との癒着も指摘された．

[1–2]　**this week's reports of a U.S. soldier executing an unarmed Iraqi**　米兵が武器を持たないイラク兵を殺害したと伝えられたこと．このほかにも，バグダッド西方のアブグレイブ刑務所（the Abu Ghraib Prizon）において，米兵が拘留したイラク兵に虐待を繰り返していた事実が写真とともに伝えられ，大きな問題となった．

[6]　**Fallujah (= Al-Fallujah)**　ファルージャ．イラク中部，バグダッド西方の都市．

[7]　**atrocity**　暴虐，非道，残虐；残虐行為，凶行．

[13]　**the Geneva Conventions**　ジュネーブ条約．1864年から数度にわたりジュネーブで開かれた国際会議で戦時中の傷病者・捕虜などの人道的扱いを協定した条約．

[17]　**insurgent**　暴徒，叛徒；（政党内の）反対分子，造反派．

[18]　**casualty**　死傷者，負傷者，死者；（一般に）被害者，損害を被った人．

cally true for the front page of the greatest newspaper in the world.

After World War II, at the Nuremberg war-crimes tribunal, they didn't go after the soldiers. They went after the German foreign minister. He was hanged. But after the My Lai massacre in Vietnam, the soldiers became the scapegoats. Semieducated, half-crazed GIs who didn't know who was going to shoot at them next carried out a massacre. That much is true. But My Lai was a tiny footnote to a major mass-murder operation called "Operation Wheeler/Wallowa," which was a search-and-destroy mission organized by nice people like us: educated Harvard graduates in air-conditioned offices. The real criminals are immune. Instead they go after some minor person about whom we can say, "He was a bad apple, not like us."

---

[2] **the Nuremberg war-crimes tribunal** ニュルンベルクでの戦犯裁判．1945–46 年，ドイツ南部バイエルン州の市ニュルンベルクで，ナチスドイツの指導者たちに対する国際軍事裁判が行なわれた．

[4] **My Lai** ミライ．ベトナム南部の小村．1968 年，米軍が住民の大量虐殺を行なった．

[10] **immune** （課税・攻撃などを）受けるおそれがない．be immune from arrest で，「逮捕される心配がない」．

Questions

1. According to Chomsky, what gave Bush the advantage in 2004?

(A) More people with money voted for him than in 2000.
(B) The "red" states were the same as the "blue" states.
(C) Voting patterns shifted slightly in four years.
(D) A lot of people felt despair and disappointment.

2. According to the article, what kind of people run U.S. elections?

(A) the kind who have a lot of knowledge about politics
(B) the kind who always worry about minorities
(C) the kind who sell toothpaste and cars
(D) the kind who believe deeply in democracy

3. Chomsky believes that

(A) the advertising industry focuses too heavily on candidates' positions
(B) George Bush is really an average guy just like you
(C) most people are more progressive than candidates of either party
(D) the Republican Party shares working-class values

4. The word "unremitting" on page 36, line 21, is closest in meaning to

(A) relentless
(B) destructive
(C) wasteful
(D) subversive

5. Chomsky says that "the battle continues" on page 36, lines 19–20. What does he mean by it?

(A) Wars like those in Iraq will go on forever unless we stop them.
(B) Every citizen has to struggle for property, but this is at least possible in America.
(C) The upper class is pessimistic about freedom and that is why we all must fight for it.
(D) Ordinary people, who form the majority, must continue to fight against the rich minority for their rights.

AMERICA AND THE WORLD

6. The word "inflated" on page 37, line 18, is closest in meaning to

(A) induced
(B) exaggerated
(C) interpreted
(D) estimated

7. The phrase "go after" on page 38, lines 2–3, is closest in meaning to

(A) find
(B) pursue
(C) care about
(D) think about

8. In talking about My Lai, Chomsky says that "The real criminals are immune." on page 38, lines 9–10. Who does he mean by "the real criminals"?

(A) the generals who planned the operation
(B) so-called bad apples like half-crazed GIs
(C) people like the German foreign minister who were hanged after the war-crimes tribunal in Nuremberg
(D) soldiers like the marine who killed an unarmed man in Fallujah

You will hear the entire text of "Hidden power." Immediately following the text, you will hear Questions 9 and 10.
Listen carefully to the text and questions, and write your answers in the space provided below.

9. _____

10. _____

Thirty years on, have no lessons been learned from Vietnam?

Roger Pulvers

introduction

国家が自分の戦争を振り返るとき、いつの時代も自国民の犠牲者数が強調して報告される。これはすべての国家に共通することであり、「正しい」国も「悪い」国も関係ないように思える。国家の指導者たちは、自国民のなかから死傷者を出してしまったのは、国家の悲劇である、と主張する。

　戦争を起こした指導者たちにすれば、こうした悲しみ方は一つの策略にすぎない。若者たち（今は男子だけでなく、女子も含まれる）を戦場に送り込む指導者たちのことを、ぼくは考えている。若者たちを嬉々として戦場に放り込むその男たちの顔には、何か特別のものがある。死神を見つめる邪悪なまなざし。そしてその男たちと死神は互いに笑みを浮かべながら見つめあっている。

　ベトナム戦争とイラク戦争を起こしたアメリカの指導者たちの口元には、まさにこの死の笑みが浮かんでいる。その唇からは重々しい哀悼のことばが吐き出されることはない。その唇には死神の笑みが浮かんでいる。世界は最後にそれを目にする。

　この記事は 2005 年 4 月 24 日付の *The Japan Times* に発表した。

This month marks the 30th anniversary of the end of the Vietnam War, a war that in Vietnam is known as the "American War."

On April 30, 1975, the government of South Vietnam surrendered to the North. The United States and its coalition of willing allies, after intervening in what was a post-colonial civil war and ravaging Vietnam on a massive scale, was finally defeated. Despite the war having produced some 2 million Vietnamese casualties during the time of U.S. involvement — and with babies being born there to this day with birth defects caused by American chemical warfare (it isn't hard to find the WMD here) — Americans, Australians and other allies have "put that war behind them."

"We've moved on from that," they say. "It's history."

This selective amnesia is not happenstance. The facts of the war in Vietnam and the record of monumental cruelty inflicted on the Vietnamese people by the American coalition have been deliberately filed away. Sure, there is talk of "mistakes." But the United States won't go back to that war: It could crimp America's style of proactive intervention in our new century, the century of the "never-ending" war on terror.

What should this very important anniversary mean to the U.S. and its allies in that unjustifiable war? [5]

It should tell the American people that they were duped by their leaders. It should tell the soldiers' families that their relatives were sent to fight (and in the case of around 70,000 Americans, to die) not in defense of American values — as Presidents Eisenhower, Kennedy, Johnson and Nixon claimed — but to impose American ideology on another nation. [10]

The final defeat in Vietnam 30 years ago should have taught Americans to study history before recklessly invading other countries. The Vietnamese people had been colonized by the French as early as the 1880s, occupied by the Japanese during World War II, then recolonized by the French until 1954. The wish of the Vietnamese people of virtually all political persuasions at that time [15] was for genuine independence and social reform. But Americans, taking up the anti-independence cause, were unable to judge the aspirations of another nation outside of the most narrow conception of American values. Take over Vietnam, give their young men lettermen's sweaters and their young women gardenia corsages for the senior prom and, gee whiz, democracy is yours for [20]

[(p.41)5]　**ravage**　荒らす，略奪する；破壊する，荒廃させる．
[(p.41)10]　**put ... behind**　(失敗などを)もう済んだことにする，忘れる．
[(p.41)12]　**amnesia**　健忘(症)，記憶消失[喪失]；自分に不都合なことを無視する[見落とす]こと．
[(p.41)12]　**happenstance**　思いもかけぬ(こと)，偶然の(できごと)．
[1]　**crimp**　妨害[じゃま]する (cramp)；(計画などを)制限を加えてつぶす．
[2]　**proactive**　先を見越して行動する[行なう]．
[5]　**unjustifiable**　道理に合わない，筋の通らない，言いわけの立たない，弁解のできない．
[6]　**dupe**　(人を)だます；(人を)だまして(...)させる．
[19]　**lettermen's sweaters**　letterman は，「大学[学校]対抗試合で優秀選手として母校の略字マーク (letter) 着用権を得た者」．したがって，そうした者が着るセーターのこと．ここでは皮肉を込めて「ベトナムの若い男性たちをアメリカ人にする」の意味で使っている．
[20]　**gardenia corsage**　アメリカの高校のダンスパーティ(以下の senior prom の注を参照)では男子が同伴した女子に「小さな花束」(corsage) を贈る．この場合は，gardenia (クチナシ)の「小さな花束」を贈ることで，「ベトナムの若い女性たちをアメリカ人のようにする」という意味で使っている．
[20]　**senior prom**　(年に1回の晴れやかな)最上級生主催のダンスパーティ．(prom は promenade.)

the asking.

The defeat in Vietnam should have taught Americans that each country has to find its own path to social equality — and that American values of liberty are not universal. Some of them, as we are now seeing in Bush's America, are barely surviving in the "homeland." [5]

If other nations wish to incorporate some fine American element of governing, they can do so in their own good time. In that very way, the people who founded the American republic borrowed grand ideas from Europe, assimilating them into an ever-changing American experience. Why don't Americans trust others to do the same? Why is it that some Americans insist on imposing [10] American institutions, so specific to American custom and mores, in every corner of the globe?

This, above all, is what America should be thinking about at the end of this month. A country's take on democracy comes from the peculiar circumstances that led to its establishment. The American social model is not the only one. [15] Japanese, Koreans, Swedes, South Africans, Indians, Venezuelans . . . they have their own traditions of dealing with social and economic inequities. Sometimes they do this better than the U.S. does; sometimes not. They don't need U.S. intervention to appreciate the difference.

Thirty years ago, the U.S. strove to impose its model on Vietnam through the [20] offices of corrupt local officials. It failed. It wasn't a mistake. It was a crime!

I was born in 1944 and the Vietnam War was the war of my generation. It is also representatives of my generation who have repeated, on a potentially more lethal scale, the very same crime in Iraq. Will they ever apologize for the

---

[(p.42)20]　**gee whiz** (= gee)　(驚き・喜び・称賛などを表わして)おや！, まあ！, これはこれは！(驚いた).

[(p.42)20–1]　**for the asking**　請求しさえすれば, 無償で (for nothing). "It's yours [there] for the asking." で「欲しいと言いさえすればもらえる」) 例 If you want to use my car, it's yours for the asking. Just let me know when you need it. (ぼくの車を使いたいなら, いつでもただで貸してあげるよ. 必要なときは言ってね.)

[8–9]　**assimilate**　(移民・文化などを)(...に)同化[融合]する, 同質化する, 溶け込ませる [into, to].

[14]　**take on...**　(...に対する)意見, 見解, 見方, 評価, 解釈, 扱い(方). a country's take on democracy で, 「民主主義に対するある一国の見解」.

[17]　**inequity**　不公正, 不公平; 不公平な事例.

[24]　**lethal**　死の; 致死の, 致命的な (fatal); (攻撃など)破壊的な.

needless killing and awful destruction that they and their allies have perpetrated on the Iraqi people?

Judging from the past it doesn't look promising. An American withdrawal will have to happen first. After that, Americans may come to know what it is like to be told by the rest of the world that they must apologize again and again. Perhaps then Americans will finally take a good hard look at their past and be mindful of it in the future. [5]

Thirty years on, have no lessons been learned from Vietnam?

Questions

1. What is WMD on page 41, line 9?

(A) Women's Movement for Democracy
(B) Weather's Mass Devastation
(C) Waste, Misery and Disaster
(D) Weapons of Mass Destruction

2. According to the author, the "selective amnesia" (on page 41, line 12) of the Americans and others was

(A) an historical accident
(B) something that the Vietnamese forgot, too
(C) due to the large number of casualties on the American side
(D) adopted on purpose

3. The sentence "It could crimp America's style of proactive intervention in our century.", on page 42, lines 1–2, can be rewritten as follows:

(A) It could help America intervene in other countries.
(B) It could encourage America to intervene in other countries.
(C) It could hamper America's ability to intervene in other countries.
(D) It could prevent America from helping other countries to be free.

4. Why does the author believe that the American people were duped?

(A) because their presidents told them that the war was being fought to defend American values
(B) because they studied history and learned about earlier wars like the one fought in Vietnam
(C) because Americans believe that some things, like lettermen's sweaters, were not suitable to life in Vietnam
(D) because Americans failed to apply American values in understanding Vietnamese aspirations

5. The author states on page 43, lines 9–10, that Americans "don't trust others to do the same." What does he mean by "to do the same"?

(A) to found a republic like the American republic
(B) to borrow certain ideas and assimilate them as they wish
(C) to assimilate American institutions and customs
(D) to abandon their own traditions in dealing with inequities

6. The word "perpetrated" on page 44, lines 1–2, can be changed to

(A) interpreted
(B) inflicted
(C) bestowed
(D) stipulated

7. According to the author, what kind of future do Americans face?

(A) one of abundance
(B) one of liberty
(C) one of hardship
(D) one of dignity

8. Which of the below titles is most suitable for this article?

(A) America Has Not Learned the Lessons of History
(B) American Values Can, if Properly Taught, Bring Social Equality
(C) Forget Vietnam, Learn the Lessons of Iraq!
(D) This is the Century of the Never-ending War on Terror

You will hear the entire text of "Thirty years on, have no lessons been learned from Vietnam?" Immediately following the text, you will hear Questions 9 and 10.
Listen carefully to the text and questions, and write your answers in the space provided below.

9. _____

10. _____

THE WORLD TODAY

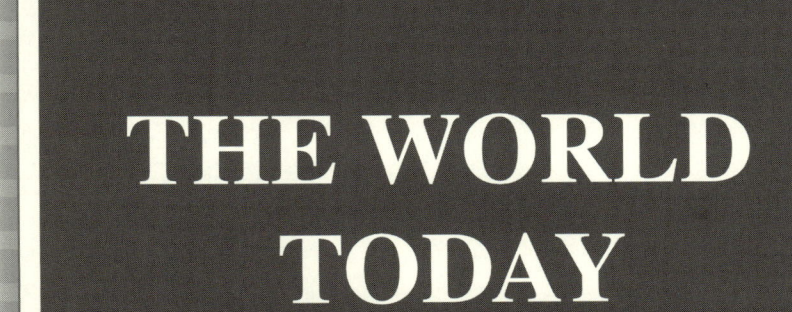

The summit that couldn't save itself

Naomi Klein

introduction

　この記事を書いた Naomi Klein は、1970 年モントリオール生まれのジャーナリスト。30 歳のときに *No Logo: Taking Aim at the Brand Bullies* (1999,『ブランドなんか、いらない 搾取で巨大化する大企業の非情』)という本を発表したが、この本は企業のイメージ戦略に対する人々の考え方を革命的に変えた。ベストセラーとなったこの *No Logo* で、クラインは、大企業はブランド・イメージによってわれわれの生活を支配している、と説いている。ブランド品を身に着けたり、その名前を口にすれば、自分たちは「トレンディでファッショナブルで自由である」と思わせることができるし、それによって消費者の意識を変えることができる。そうやってわれわれにブランド品をもっともっと買わせようとするのだ。彼女はこのように論じている。

　ナオミ・クラインは、ノーム・チョムスキー(本テキストの AMERICA AND THE WORLD の "Hidden power" を参照のこと)と同じで、普通の人たちの力 (people power) を信じようとする。

　この記事は 2002 年 9 月 4 日付のイギリスの新聞 *The Guardian* に発表されたものであるが、クラインはまさにそのような視点から、同年にヨハネスブルグで開催された地球サミットを見つめている。

When Rio hosted the first earth summit in 1992, there was so much goodwill surrounding the event that it was nicknamed, without irony, the Summit to Save the World. This week in Johannesburg, nobody has claimed that the follow-up World Summit on Sustainable Development could save the world. The question has been whether the summit could even save itself. [5]

The sticking point has been what UN bureaucrats call "implementation" and the rest of us call "doing something". Much of the blame for the "implementation gap" has been placed at the doorstep of the US. It was George W Bush who abandoned the only significant environmental regulations that came out of the Rio conference: the Kyoto protocol on climate change. It was Bush who [10] decided not to come to Johannesburg, signalling that the issues being discussed here — from basic sanitation to clean energy — are low priorities for his administration. And the US delegation has blocked all proposals that involve either directly regulating multinational corporations or dedicating significant new funds to sustainable development.

But the Bush-bashing is too easy: the summit hasn't failed because of anything that happened in Johannesburg. It has failed because the entire process was booby-trapped from the start. [5]

When Canadian entrepreneur and diplomat Maurice Strong was appointed to chair the Rio summit, his vision was of a gathering that brought all the "stakeholders" to the table — not just governments, but also environmentalists, indigenous groups and lobby groups, as well as multinational corporations. [10]

Strong's vision allowed for more participation from civil society than any previous UN conference, at the same time as it raised unprecedented amounts of corporate funds for the summit. But the sponsorship had a price. Corporations came to Rio with clear conditions: they would embrace ecologically sustainable practices, but only voluntarily, through non-binding codes and [15] "best practice" partnerships with NGOs and governments. In other words, when the business sector came to the table in Rio, direct regulation of business was pushed off.

In Johannesburg, these "partnerships" have passed into self-parody, with the conference centre chock-a-block with displays for BMW "clean cars" and [20] billboards for De Beers diamonds announcing "Water is Forever". The summit's

---

[(p.48)4] **World Summit on Sustainable Development** 持続可能な開発に関する世界首脳会議. 2002年8〜9月に南アフリカ・ヨハネスブルグで開催された，地球サミット(WSSD，リオプラス10サミットとも呼ばれる)のこと．1992年にブラジル・リオデジャネイロで開かれたリオ地球サミットは，「持続可能な開発」(Sustainable Development)をキーワードに地球環境問題と開発問題を取り上げた史上最大の国際会議であり，また京都議定書の前身である気候変動枠組み条約が締結された会合だった．ヨハネスブルグでのサミットは，それから10年後に開催された．

[(p.48)8] **at the doorstep of...** 人の責任［せい］に．at the door of...，あるいは，at a person's door とも言う．"He laid the fault at her door." で，「彼はその過失を彼女の責任にした」．例 If you have problems with money, don't lay them on my doorstep [don't place them at my doorstep].（カネの問題があるとしても，俺のせいにするなよ.）

[5] **booby-trap** …にまぬけ落としを仕掛ける；…に偽装爆弾［地雷］を仕掛ける；策略・陰謀・わなにかける．

[20] **chock-a-block** chockablock ともつづる．

[21] **De Beers** (= De Beers Conslidated Mines) デビアス・コンソリデーテッド・マインズ(社)（〜 Ltd.）．南アフリカに本拠をもつ世界最大のダイヤモンド会社．1888年創立．

THE WORLD TODAY

chief sponsor was Eskom, South Africa's soon-to-be-privatised national energy company. A recent study stated that under Eskom's restructuring, 40,000 households are losing access to electricity each month.

This cuts to the heart of the real debate about the summit. The World Business Council for Sustainable Development, a corporate lobby group founded in Rio, insists the route to sustainability is the same trickle-down formula being imposed by the WTO and IMF: poor countries must make themselves hospitable to foreign investment, usually by privatising basic services, from water to electricity to healthcare. [5]

But post-Enron, it's hard to believe that companies can be trusted to keep their own books, let alone save the world. And unlike a decade ago, the economic model of laissez-faire development is being rejected by popular movements around the world. [10]

This time, many of the "stakeholders" weren't at the official table, but out in the streets, or organising counter-summit conferences to plot very different routes to development: debt cancellation, an end to the privatisation of water [15]

---

[1] **Eskom** エスコム社．本文中にもあるとおり．民営化が予定されている南アフリカエネルギー会社．南アの大半のエネルギーを創出．

[1] **privatise** （企業などを）民営化する．この記事はイギリスの *The Guardian* 紙に掲載されたものなので，イギリス式スペルになっている．15 行目の organising, 16 行目の privatisation にも注意．

[4–5] **the World Business Council for Sustainable Development**（= **WBCSD**）持続可能な発展［開発］のための世界経済人会議，世界環境経済人会議．1992 年発足．

[6] **trickle-down formula** トリクルダウン理論の［による］．政府資金を大企業に流入させると，それが中小企業と消費者に及び景気を刺激するという理論．

[7] **WTO**（= **the World Trade Organization**）世界貿易機関．GATT を引き継いで 1995 年に発足した国連の関連機関．

[7] **IMF**（= **the International Monetary Fund**）国際通貨基金．為替相場の安定を図ることを目的に設立された国連の専門機関．本部は Washington, D.C. にある．1945 年発足．

[10] **Enron** エンロン．2001 年に倒産したテキサス州ヒューストン市のエネルギー会社．史上最大の倒産であり，米国の政財界を揺るがせた．

[10–11] **keep their own books** keep the books で「帳簿をつける」．したがって，「企業各社が帳簿をつける」．

[12] **laissez-faire** （経済学で）自由放任主義，レッセフェール．政府がその役割を法と秩序の維持だけにとどめ，経済活動は民間の自由に任せれば，市場機構が機能して，資源の最適配分が達成され，経済厚生は最大になるという考え方．発音にも注意（/lèseɪféə(r),-fǽə(r), lèɪ-, -zèɪ-/）．Z は黙字．

and electricity, reparations for apartheid abuses, affordable housing, land reform.

These movements are no longer willing simply to talk about their demands; they are acting on them. In the past two years, South Africa has experienced a surge in direct action, with groups organising to resist evictions, claim unproductive land and reconnect cut-off water and electricity in the townships.

The fact that a world summit on poverty has been unfolding in their backyard has also created serious obstacles. Sandton, the ultra-rich suburb where the conference is being held, has been transformed into a military zone. There have been arrests and police attacks on protest marches. On Monday, at a pro-Palestinian demonstration staged outside a speech by Shimon Peres, the Israeli Foreign Minister, soldiers fired rubber bullets and water cannon, severely injuring several protesters.

The World Summit on Sustainable Development isn't going to save the world; it merely offers an exaggerated mirror of it. In the gourmet restaurants of Sandton, delegates have dined out on their concern for the poor. Outside the gates, poor people have been hidden away, assaulted and imprisoned for what has become the iconic act of resistance in an unsustainable world: refusing to disappear.

---

[8]　**Sandton**　サンドトン．ヨハネスブルグ郊外の町．ビジネス街，ショッピング街があり，高級ホテルが立ち並ぶ．
[12]　**rubber bullet**　（暴動鎮圧用）のゴム弾．
[12]　**water cannon**　（デモ隊などを散らす放水車の）放水砲．

THE WORLD TODAY

Questions

1. The phrase "sticking point" on page 48, line 6, can NOT be changed to

(A) deadlock
(B) impasse
(C) hold up
(D) deadline

2. The author blames George W. Bush for

(A) not adopting the Kyoto protocol on climate change
(B) giving priority to issues like clean energy over sanitation
(C) agreeing with UN bureaucrats that "implementation" is the problem
(D) dedicating significant new funds to sustainable development

3. What had corporations decided to do at Rio?

(A) pay the price for sponsorships by using corporate funds
(B) give in to direct regulation of business
(C) participate in civil society as Maurice Strong directed
(D) not go along with binding codes and "best practice" partnerships with NGOs and governments

4. The phrase "clock-a-block with" on page 49, line 20, can be changed to

(A) filled with
(B) emptied of
(C) represented by
(D) satisfied with

5. Who was the main sponsor of the Johannesburg summit?

(A) De Beers
(B) Eskom
(C) BMW
(D) Enron

6. The author believes that making poor countries hospitable to foreign investment is

(A) an admirable formula for sustainability
(B) an important part of what is known as "direct action"
(C) not a particularly desirable policy
(D) not included in the economic model of laissez-faire development

7. According to the author, there were two world summits in Johannesburg. What was the "other one"?

(A) businesses and corporations making plans of their own
(B) people, groups and organizations demonstrating in the streets
(C) politicians like the Israeli foreign minister making policy speeches
(D) the World Business Council for Sustainable Development, in conjunction with the WTO and IMF

8 The word "iconic" on page 51, line 18, is closest in meaning to

(A) revolutionary
(B) progressive
(C) symbolic
(D) ironic

You will hear the entire text of "The summit that couldn't save itself." Immediately following the text, you will hear Questions 9 and 10.
Listen carefully to the text and questions, and write your answers in the space provided below.

9.

10.

A new kind of challenge

Fareed Zakaria

Introduction

　アメリカは中国のことで頭を悩ませつつある。ちょうど 80 年代に日本のことで頭を悩ませていたように。しかし、今回はあのときとはまったく話が違う。80 年代、アメリカは日本の経済成長に脅威を感じていた（今はそんなことはないが）。しかし、今は中国に対して軍事・政治的に恐怖を抱いている。少なくとも、中国は今後どのような方向に進むのか、脅威を感じている。

　Newsweek 国際版の 2005 年 5 月 9 日号に掲載された Fareed Zakaria のこの記事は、中国の国内発展を考えた政府の短期・長期計画とあわせて、同国が台湾や日本やアメリカをどのように見ているかについて論じている。

　中国がはたしてどのような変貌を遂げるのか、予測はできない。しかし、明らかに言えるのは、今後アメリカは中国の動きから決して目を離すことはないだろう、ということだ。中国はさらなる発展を遂げるだろうし、それを目の当たりにしながらアメリカはますます頭を悩ますことになるだろう。

For the first decade of its development (the 1980s), China did not have a foreign policy. Or rather, its grand strategy was a growth strategy. China quietly supported (or did not oppose) U.S. policies, largely because it saw good relations with America as the cornerstone of its development push. And this nonconfrontational approach still lingers. With the exception of anything related to Taiwan, even now its major foreign-policy moves are largely outgrowths of economic imperatives. These days that means a ceaseless search for continued supplies of oil and other commodities. [5]

But things are changing. In a paper titled "The Beijing Consensus," drawing heavily on interviews with leading Chinese officials and academics, Joshua Cooper Ramo provides a fascinating picture of China's new foreign policy. "Rather than building a US-style power, bristling with arms and intolerant of others' world views," he writes, "China's emerging power is based on the example of their own model, the strength of their economic system, and their rigid defense of . . . national sovereignty." [10]

China has followed a very different development strategy than Japan. Rather [15]

A new kind of challenge

than focusing only on export-led growth to a few markets and keeping its internal market closed, China opened itself to foreign investment and trade. The result is that much of the world now relies on the China market. From the United States to Germany to Japan, exports to China are among the crucial factors propelling growth. For developing markets, China is the indispensable [5] trading partner.

In November 2004, President George W. Bush and China's President Hu Jintao traveled through Asia. I was in the region a few weeks afterward and was struck by how almost everyone I spoke with rated Hu's visits as far more successful than Bush's. Karim Raslan, a Malaysian writer, explained: "Bush [10] talked obsessively about terror. He sees all of us through that one prism. Yes, we worry about terror, but frankly that's not the sum of our lives. We have many other problems. We're retooling our economies, we're wondering how to deal with the rise of China, we're trying to address health, social and environmental problems. Hu talked about all this; he talked about our agenda, not just [15] his agenda." From Indonesia to Brazil, China is winning new friends.

There are a group of Americans — chiefly neoconservatives and Pentagon officials — who have been sounding the alarms about the Chinese threat. And they speak of it largely in military terms, usually wildly exaggerating China's capabilities. But the facts simply do not support their case. China is certainly [20] expanding its military, with a budget that rises 10 percent or more a year. But it is still spending a fraction of what America does, at most 10 percent of the Pentagon's annual bill.

The Chinese threat or challenge will not present itself in the familiar guise of

---

[(p.54)10–11] **Ramo, Joshua Cooper** アメリカで活躍する中国人のジャーナリスト．*Time* 誌の外国人エディターとしても活躍した．著書に，*No Visible Horizon: Surviving the World's Most Dangerous Sport* (2003) がある．

[7–8] **Hu Jintao** (1942–) 胡錦濤（フーチンタオ，こきんとう）．中国の国家主席（2003 年から）．

[15] **agenda** 「予定表，計画表，（会議用の）議事日程，会議事項」のことだが，よく次のような使われ方をする．例 Ishihara talks about peace, but he has a different agenda.（石原はよく「平和」を口にするが，実は別のことを企んでいる．）例 My agenda is simply that I want to graduate. I'm not trying to curry favor with the teacher by giving him a present.（ぼくはただ卒業したいだけだ．先生に貢物をしてご機嫌を取るなんてことはしないさ．）

[19] **exaggerate** (...を)大げさに言う，誇張する；強調しすぎる．

another Soviet Union, straining to keep pace with America in military terms. It is more likely to be what Ramo describes as an "asymmetrical superpower." It will use its economic dominance and its political skills to achieve its objectives. China does not want to invade and occupy Taiwan; it is more likely to keep undermining the Taiwan independence movement, so that Beijing slowly [5] accumulates advantage and wears out the opponent. "The goal for China is not conflict but the avoidance of conflict," Ramo writes. "True success in strategic issues involves manipulating a situation so effectively that the outcome is inevitably in favor of Chinese interests. This emerges from the oldest Chinese strategic thinker, Sun Zi, who argued that 'every battle is won or lost before it [10] is ever fought'."

At least that's the plan. The trouble is that while maintaining this long-term strategy, China often lapses into short-term behavior that seems aggressive and hostile. Perhaps this is because the rational decision-making that guides its economic policy is not so easily applied in the realm of politics, where honor, [15] history, pride and anger all play a large role. So with Taiwan, last week Beijing was playing out its long-term plan, "normalizing" relations with the island's main opposition party, and smothering it with conciliation. But last month it passed the anti-secession law, which angered most Taiwanese and alarmed Americans and Europeans. [20]

Or take its relations with Japan. It makes little sense for Beijing to behave as aggressively as it does with Tokyo. It only ensures that China will have a hostile neighbor, one with an economy that is still four times its size. A wiser strategy might be to keep ensnaring Japan with economic ties and cooperation, achieving dominance over time. [25]

---

[1]　**strain to**　懸命に努める，懸命になる．
[2]　**asymmetrical**（= **asymmetric**）　不釣り合いの．
[3]　**dominance**　優勢，優位，優越．
[10]　**Sun Zi**（= **Sun Tsu**）　孫子．孫子の『孫子兵法』は *The Art of Sun Tsu* として，西洋諸国でも広く読まれている．
[13]　**lapse into**　（罪悪などに）陥る，堕落する；[ある状態に]なる．
[24]　**ensnare**　わなにかける，陥れる；誘惑する．例 Helmut tried to ensnare Makiko by promising her riches, but she could tell right away he was lying.（ヘルムートは，きっとお金持ちにするから，と言って真紀子を陥れようとしたが，それは嘘だとすぐに彼女はわかった．）

A new kind of challenge

There are grounds for reconciliation. Japanese have not behaved perfectly, but they have apologized several times for their wartime aggression. They have given China more than $34 billion in development aid (effectively reparations), something never mentioned by the Chinese. Even in this latest standoff, the Japanese moved first to break the impasse. [5]

But for China, emotion seems to get in the way. Having abandoned communism, the Communist Party has been using nationalism as the glue that keeps China together. And modern Chinese nationalism is defined in large part by its hostility toward Japan. Mao is still a hero in China despite his many catastrophic policies because he unified the country and fought the Japanese. And [10] as China advances economically, Chinese nationalism only gets more intense. Scratch a Shanghai Yuppie and you will find a virulent nationalist — on Taiwan, Japan and America.

Beijing assumes it can handle popular sentiments but it might well be wrong. After all, it does not have much experience in it, not being a democracy. It [15] deals with public anger and emotions cagily, unsure whether to encourage them or clamp down for fear of where they might lead. So it does not know what to do with a group like the Patriots Alliance, an Internet-based hypernationalist group that has organized the biggest demonstrations in the country in six years. [20]

Experts say that the Chinese Communist Party has been seriously discussing

---

[3–4] **reparations** （複数形で）補償金，賠償金．
[4] **this latest standoff** 最近の日中間の緊張関係．この記事が書かれた 2005 年 5 月にも中国では大規模な反日デモが行なわれた．
[6] **get in the way** （人の）じゃまになる［をする］．例 Japanese kanji are so difficult they get in the way of foreigners trying to learn the language.（日本語の漢字はあまりに難しく，それが外国人の日本語習得をむずかしくしている．）
[7] **glue** にかわ；接着剤．
[9] **Mao Zedong**（1893–1976） 毛沢東．1943 年から中国共産党中央委員会主席，1949 年中華人民共和国成立とともに初代国家主席を務めた．
[18] **the Patriots Alliance** 愛国者同盟網．インターネットを通じて反日運動を呼びかけている中国の愛国者団体．戦時中の日本の戦略行為などを厳しく告発する記事が多数掲載されたこの団体のサイトを見て，多くの中国国民が反日デモに参加したといわれる．中国政府はこのサイトを一時閉鎖した．

THE WORLD TODAY

political reforms and studying dominant single parties from Sweden to Singapore, to understand how it might maintain its position in a more open political system. "The smartest people in the government are studying these issues," a well-placed Beijing resident told me. But politics is often about more than smarts. In any event, how Beijing's mandarins end up handling their own [5] people might have much to do with how China ends up handling the world.

[4]　**well-placed**　よい地位にいる；高い地位にある．
[5]　**smarts**　ここでは being smart の意味で使われている．
[5]　**mandarin**　(中国の清朝の)上級官吏，マンダリン；陰の実力者と目される高官，有力な官僚；保守的官公吏．

A new kind of challenge

Questions

1. The word "lingers" on page 54, line 5, is closest in meaning to

(A) causes problems
(B) angers
(C) remains
(D) is bothersome

2. The word "ceaseless" on page 54, line 7, is closest in meaning to

(A) constant
(B) serious
(C) underhanded
(D) gradual

3. According to Karim Raslan, Hu's visit in Asia was more successful than Bush's because

(A) Hu seemed truly interested in terror and its consequences
(B) China is retooling its economy like other Asian countries
(C) Bush spoke too much about the rise of China
(D) Hu seemed more interested in the problems of the countries he was visiting

4. The author states, "The facts do not support their case." on page 55, line 20. By "their case" the author means

(A) neoconservatives and Pentagon officials claiming that China spends a fraction of what America does on arms
(B) Chinese who claim that their military capabilities are certainly expanding
(C) Chinese who claim that China spends at most 10 percent of what America does on its military
(D) neoconservatives and Pentagon officials claiming that China is very strong militarily

5. How would you compare the military budgets of China and the United States?

(A) The military budget of China is about ten times that of the U.S.
(B) The two military budgets are roughly the same.
(C) The military budget of the U.S. is about one-tenth the size of that of China.
(D) The military budget of the U.S. is about ten times that of China.

6. What does the author mean by "achieving dominance over time" on page 56, line 25?

(A) attain a superior position in the course of years
(B) conquer time with clever policies
(C) allow Japan to be powerful in the long run
(D) establish an equal relationship over the years

7. The author states that "Beijing assumes it can handle popular sentiments" on page 57, line 14. What does he mean by popular sentiments?

(A) opinion about China all over the world
(B) public opinion in China
(C) anger against China in countries like Japan and the U.S.
(D) ideas about economic growth that are supported by the Communist Party

8. The word "cagily" on page 57, line 16, is closest in meaning to

(A) intentionally
(B) gladly
(C) carefully
(D) dangerously

You will hear the entire text of "A new kind of challenge." Immediately following the text, you will hear Questions 9 and 10.
Listen carefully to the text and questions, and write your answers in the space provided below.

9.

10.

Memories are made of . . . history managed and manipulated?

Roger Pulvers

Introduction

ぼくが最初に訪れた異国の地は、旧ソビエト連邦だった。当時ぼくはまだ20歳になったばかりで、UCLAでロシア語を勉強していた。その頃のぼくはまったく純真なアメリカ青年で、何かでかいことをしてやろうという野心に満ち溢れていた。初めての海外旅行でソ連に行くというのは、ある意味変わったことだったかもしれない。メキシコやイギリスやフランスやイタリアに行った友人がほとんどだったから。

これは2005年の5月に *The Japan Times* に寄稿した記事だが、そこに書いたように、ぼくが初めてソ連を訪れた1964年は、第二次世界大戦終結からまだ19年しか経っていなかった。ソ連からはるか遠く離れたアメリカのロサンゼルスに育ったぼくにすれば、あの戦争は一連の物語としか思えなかった。小説や映画のなかの話としか考えられなかった。しかし、そのとき初めてソ連を訪れてみて、ぼくははっきり思い知らされた。戦争は、まったく想像できないものであり、残酷で、みにくく、まるで意味のないことなのだ。およそ人間のすることとは思えない、非常にひどいことなのだ。

歴史を改ざんして、戦争は意味あることである、それはすばらしいことだ、などと言うのは、戦争を起こすのと同じぐらい、罪深いことである。

Way back in 1964 and 1965 I made extended trips to and around the Soviet Union. Memories that are 40 years old are hard enough to relate to the reality of the present, let alone when they are of a country that has ceased to exist. This, though, is precisely what I aim to do.

Being able to speak Russian, I traveled about with considerable freedom [5] from Moscow, Leningrad and Novgorod in the north to Kiev, Kharkov and the lovely Crimean port town of Yalta in the south. I found a country that was multiracial and multicultural, despite the efforts of the government's cynical technocrats to suppress such variety. But wherever I went, I was greeted with a singular, almost obsessive, barrage of opinion. Everyone seemed to feel obliged [10] to talk to me about World War II and their own or their family's experience of it.

I was reminded of these encounters by the upcoming anniversary of the end of that war. On May 8, it will be 60 years since Germany's Nazi-led government surrendered unconditionally to the Allied Forces. But when I was racing about the USSR in the summer of 1964, only 19 years had passed since then. There wasn't a single person in their mid-20s or over who didn't appear deeply affected by the German invasion of their country. [5]

Anniversaries, of course, come naturally with the passage of time — but that does not mean they are unstaged or unmanipulated as events. The D-Day celebrations last year, marking 60 years since the Allies landed on the beaches of Normandy, provided, at least for the winning side, an opportunity for Americans, Canadians, British people and Australians, among others, to mark their [10] massive and courageous contribution to the defeat of fascism in Europe. (Judging by the coverage of those celebrations in the U.S. press, however, with its scant mention of non-American troops at Normandy, you would not be blamed for thinking that the United States singlehandedly took on and defeated the Third Reich.) [15]

Why, I remember wondering on those two journeys around the Soviet Union long ago, are these people so haunted by the war? It was almost as if the entire country was still gripped by a siege mentality.

It dawned on me as I spoke with teachers, coalminers, engineers, farmers, retirees. In my studies in schools in the U.S., I had never been taught about the [20] stupendous sacrifices made by the people of the USSR. I, too, had thought that the country of my birth, the United States, had saved the day in a kind of Superman rescue for which all Europeans would be eternally grateful.

I learned on my trips that more than 25 million Soviet soldiers and civilians were killed as a direct result of the German invasion. This is more than the [25] combined total of dead of all the other countries, on both sides of the war. I also learned that more than 70 percent of German soldiers who died during the war

---

[(p.61)9]　**technocrat**　テクノクラート．政治経済や科学技術について高度の専門的知識を持つ行政官・管理者．技術官僚．

[(p.61)10]　**barrage**　（打撃・質問の）連続，集中，雨．a barrage of questions で「やつぎばやの質問」．

[7]　**unstage** ⇔ stage.

[7]　**unmanipulate** ⇔ manipulate.

[18]　**siege mentality**　被包囲心理(自分が常に攻撃[抑圧]にさらされていると感じる精神状態)．

[21]　**stupendous**　途方もない，大変な．

are buried within the borders of the former Soviet Union.

Hitler's war was primarily a war against eastern communism, not western capitalism. (Fascists and capitalists have always been in each other's pockets.) The Nazi-led government had little interest in wrenching colonies away from western European powers. The Nazis' goal was to "liberate" the peoples of the Soviet Union from the yoke of communism, which they considered a Russian-driven ideology used to secure a Russian-dominated empire.

Even as Germany's defeat became evident to Hitler and his remaining loyal generals, they would have gladly made a separate pact with the Allies invading from the west to repel the Allies invading from the east, namely the Red Army, to keep the latter from the gates of Berlin. Gen. Dwight D. Eisenhower wouldn't have a bar of this, and on May 7, 1945, the document of surrender was signed. Fighting ceased the next day at 11:01 p.m. The German capital was duly partitioned, shaping the world order for the next 44 years.

But war anniversaries are meaningless unless we try to put them in a perspective that will help us prevent the reoccurrence of mass carnage. It is not enough to gloat over our heroism, however genuine, or to lord our victory over the defeated.

The Russian people, who bore the full brunt of the German invasion, were never again going to allow themselves to be surrounded by enemies. The siege

---

[6]　**yoke** [**the ~**]　（暴君などの）支配，圧迫；（奴隷などの）束縛（状態），隷属．groan under the yoke of slavery で，「奴隷の苦役に苦しむ」．例 The people of Africa lived under the yoke of colonialism for centuries.（アフリカの人たちは，何世紀も植民地主義の支配下にあった．）

[9]　**pact**　協定，条約．

[11–12]　**wouldn't [won't] have a bar of ...**　...には我慢がならない，...は大嫌いだ．もともとはオーストラリアの口語表現であったが，今ではイギリスでも普通に使われる．例 Jim wanted Rumiko to have some marijuana but she wouldn't have a bar of it.（ジムは留美子に大麻を勧めたが，彼女はそういうのは大嫌いだ［きっぱり断った］．）

[15–16]　**in (a) perspective**　全体の視野で；真相を正しく．see [look at] things in (their proper) perspective で，「釣り合いの取れた物の見方をする」という意味になる．例 "Look at it in perspective," Alice told Fiona. "You failed biology, but that unit doesn't count toward your degree anyway."（「バランス良く物事を見なくちゃ」とアリスはフィオナに言った．「生物学は落としちゃったかもしれないけど，その単位は学位に関係ないわ」）

[17]　**gloat**　さも満足そうに［いい気味だと思って］眺める，ほくそえむ (on, over)．

[19]　**brunt**　（攻撃の）ほこさき；苛酷な局面．

THE WORLD TODAY

mentality, with all of its distrust of outsiders, was a natural outgrowth of the war, and it was nurtured by the Soviet government long after the peace was brokered. The great majority of Soviet citizens accepted the Communist Party's hold over government because they felt it was the only thing that could protect them from another invasion from the west. [5]

The country called the Soviet Union may no longer exist, but Russians, still mindful of the monumental losses they suffered in what they call the "Great Patriotic War," are anxiety-prone: they fear being surrounded by unfriendly governments. (This is something they share with Americans, who are ready to invade their neighbors to the south at the drop of a hat if they sense serious hostility there.) [10]

This is what comes to mind at the time of this anniversary. A time for celebration, yes. But also a time to recall what really happened and use that recollection to inform the present.

Isolating Russia, rather than engaging it, will only feed the fears of the past. [15]

---

[3]　**broker**　調停する.

[10]　**at the drop of a hat**　ちょっとした合図で，待ってましたとばかりに，いそいそと，すぐに，すぐさま，たちまち，だしぬけに.

Memories are made of ... history managed and manipulated?

> Questions

1. Bearing in mind that this article was written in May 2005, when were the D-Day 60th anniversary celebrations held?

   (A) 2004
   (B) 2003
   (C) 2000
   (D) 1995

2. According to the author, on his trip to the USSR in 1964

   (A) not many people over about 25 seemed influenced by the German invasion
   (B) everyone over about 25 seemed influenced by the German invasion
   (C) single people over about 25 seemed influenced by the German invasion
   (D) no single people over about 25 seemed influenced by the German invasion

3. "Scant mention" on page 62, line 13, means

   (A) almost nobody talking about something
   (B) virtually constantly talking about something
   (C) people not crediting the United States for the defeat of Germany
   (D) the U.S. press celebrating the victory in a big way

4. Which of the following is closest in meaning to the phrase "It dawned on me" on page 62, line 19?

   (A) I realized
   (B) I happened to forget
   (C) I never really understood
   (D) I woke up early and saw

5. About how many Soviet people were killed during World War II?

   (A) 250,000
   (B) 2,500,000
   (C) 25,000,000
   (D) 250,000,000

6. Which of the following is closest in meaning to the expression "wrenching away" on page 63, line 4?

(A) putting away
(B) taking away
(C) staying away
(D) doing away with

7. According to the author, the Nazi-led government

(A) was very interested in taking over the colonies of western European powers
(B) was not particularly interested in taking over the colonies of western European powers
(C) was very interested in securing communism in a Russian-dominated empire
(D) was not particularly interested in securing communism in a Russian-dominated empire

8. The author considers war anniversaries

(A) not meaningful because they create heroes
(B) meaningful only if they help us prevent new wars
(C) meaningful because they signify victory over the defeated
(D) meaningful because they prevent carnage

You will hear the entire text of "Memories are made of . . . history managed and manipulated?" Immediately following the text, you will hear Questions 9 and 10. Listen carefully to the text and questions, and write your answers in the space provided below.

9. _____

10. _____

JAPAN

Where do the Japanese stand today?

Roger Pulvers

introduction

　この記事は 2000 年に書いたものであるが、日本はその頃もなお「失われた 10 年」（lost decade）にはまり込んでしまっていて、経済も政治も停滞期から抜け出せないでいた。そしてその停滞期はさらに拡大し、今や 15 年にも及ぼうとしている。あの 10 年は、「日本でもっとも長い 10 年」になってしまった。

　この記事でぼくが指摘するのは、日本人は、何か社会に問題が起こると、すぐに政治家や閣僚を批判する、ということである。日本人が政府の政策を批判するときにいちばんよく口にするのは、「なんとかしてもらいたいです」ではないだろうか。

　しかし、「誰に」なんとかしてもらったのだろう？　日本人が「自分がそれをなんとかしたいです」と言うようなことははたしてあるだろうか？　民主主義においては、最終的な決定を下すのは、政治家の気まぐれ（whim）ではなく、人々の意志（will）なのだ。少なくとも、それが民主主義の論理だ。

　論理上の民主主義は、民主主義とは言えない。国民一人ひとりの積極的な政治参加がなければ、それは絶対に成り立たない。はたして日本国民にその腹づもりができているだろうか？

A malaise is abroad in Japan and that malaise is apathy and hopelessness. Ever since the Meiji Era — 1868–1912 — when the modern state of Japan was established and developed, the one thing that the Japanese people imbued their national effort, their prodigious diligence, with was a sense of hope: that little by little the country could and would be improved and strengthened, that [5] it was possible for a non-European nation to thrive and prosper.

　American hope was based on personal aggrandizement, the sense that you contributed to your country's welfare by ensuring your own. But Japanese hope was founded on the notion of communal aggrandizement, where the commune is taken as the entire nation. Personal pride stemmed from how [10] much you contributed to the whole without making undue demands on the common bounty.

　The fact is that for the first time in nearly 150 years, this foundation, in its ethical and practical makeup, is breaking apart. Japan has entered a period of profound social transition. What will the new structure look like? And more [15] critically for the Japanese themselves, what will it be like to inhabit it?

The primary goal of the people of Meiji was to catch up with and overtake the West at its own game. That game was called empire. The Japanese wanted to join the Kaiser's club, to stake out parts of Asia for itself as the Western powers had done; and they were not averse to turning the trappings of idealistic Meiji nationalism toward cynical and sinister aims. [5]

The early strategy of conquer and possess of the Showa era, the first part of which ran from the mid-'20s until the mid-'40s, led to defeat at the hands of the Allies in August 1945, and the Japanese people set their collective mind in the latter years of the era on a more valid, if related, goal. Why should the West, [10] they argued, have a monopoly on prosperity? If we can only buckle down and work as one united nation to foster economic growth, they figured, then we can achieve the goal of Meiji, enter the first-world club and we won't have to subjugate other populations to do it.

It all seemed the indisputable national ethos and, moreover, it worked. The [15] Japanese miracle was recognized and applauded by the world. Developing countries looked to the Japanese model, as opposed to the European or American ones, as the epitome of collective aspiration. On television talk shows in

---

[(p.68)1] **malaise** 不定愁訴; 不安, 不調, 倦怠(感).
[(p.68)3] **imbue** (感情・意見などを)(人・心に)吹き込む.(通例受身で用いられる.)
[(p.68)4] **prodigious** 巨大な, 莫大な, 桁はずれの.
[(p.68)7] **aggrandizement** (富・地位などの)増大, 強化. personal aggrandizement で, 出世, 栄達.
[(p.68)10] **stem** [...から]生じる, 起こる, 由来する. "His failure stems from his carelessness." で,「彼の失敗の原因は不注意だ」. 例 Jack's inability to speak Japanese stems from his total lack of interest in languages. (ジャックが日本語が全然しゃべれないのは, ことばというものにまったく興味がないからさ.)
[(p.68)11] **undue** 過度の, はなはだしい; 不当な, 不適当な.
[(p.68)12] **bounty** 恵み深さ, 気前よさ, 寛大.
[5] **averse** 嫌って, 反対して (to). 例 I'm not averse to a good glass of wine once in a while. (たまにはワインもいいな.)
[11] **monopoly** 独占, 専有.
[14] **subjugate** 征服する, 服従[隷属]させる (to).
[15] **indisputable** 争う余地のない (unquestionable), 明白な, 確実な.
[15] **ethos** (一国民・一社会・一制度などの)気風, 精神, 民族[社会]精神, 風潮, エトス.
[16] **applaud** 拍手かっさいする; ほめる.
[18] **epitome** [the 〜] (...の)典型, 縮図.

the 1980s, Japan was presented as the ideal state in which happy, problem-free people toiled selflessly and freely in the interests of the public, and hence their personal, well-being . . . until it all seemed to crumble in the early '90s and everyone, from political leaders to ordinary citizens, began asking the single question to which no one had an answer: Where did it all go wrong? [5]

The metaphor chosen by Japan to describe its economy in the 1980s was that of the bubble. It was a time when a modest area of land in the Tokyo metropolitan area was said to be worth more than California. A friend of mine, a senior planner in the Japanese government, devised a plan for Japan to buy the state of Montana. I thought it was a great idea myself, although I was obliged to point [10] out that Montana was, in fact, owned by lots of different people and it might be hard to coordinate a sale.

Japanese were buying the sexiest overseas assets — golf courses in California, landmark skyscrapers in New York, prime coastal land in Queensland, Australia — for hideously inflated sums. This was the equivalent of the Roaring [15] '20s in America. The fishmonger at my local fish shop sported a Louis Vuitton apron for gutting his garfish . . . and yet he still could afford neither the time nor the money to take a decent vacation with his family.

The bubble that burst around a decade ago was no bubble at all. The image was a con, for the benefits that it brought were surely not spread evenly [20] throughout the society; and the consumption frenzy that it engendered left essential areas of the economy, personal and corporate, neglected and vulnerable to degradation and rot.

As the air drained out and the proverbial bubble shriveled, firms were left

---

[2] **toil** （長時間）骨を折って働く，苦労する
[3] **crumble** ぼろぼろにくずれる，砕ける．
[13] **asset** （通例複数形で）資産，財産．
[15] **hideously** おそろしく，すさまじく．
[20] **con** ペテン，詐欺．
[21] **frenzy** 狂乱，熱狂；逆上，乱心．
[23] **degradation** （名誉・地位などの）低落，下落；悪化，低下．
[23] **rot** 腐れ，腐敗．
[24] **proverbial** ことわざの，ことわざにある．この場合は，「よく知られた，かの有名な」．例 Rick had to manage with the proverbial "teenage son" problem when his 16-year-old son, George, was arrested for speeding. (リックはいわゆる「10代の息子」問題で頭を抱えていた．彼の16歳の息子のジョージが，スピード違反で現行犯逮捕されたんだよ．)

with massive debt, highly questionable accounting practices and, in some cases, shoddy quality control. All of these defects had to be airbrushed over in the interests of what was slowly coming to be seen not as the Japanese model but rather as the Japanese myth. Naturally, however, the politicians, whose financial and moral base came from the overly-subsidized countryside and the heavily protected manufacturing elite of the larger cities, were convinced that the essential pattern of national growth forged in Meiji and refined in late Showa was not flawed. All you have to do, they believed, was "retie your loincloth," as the phrase goes, and sweat it out. Japan, once again, would stand up and conquer.

This, alas, did not happen. The politicians responded by not only repeatedly retying their loincloths until the fat men all but lost their voices but also by digging in their heels. They are still trying to prop up the old edifice by pouring on concrete to maintain its outward appearance. The result is walls that are heavier and more prone to collapse. The Japanese people have always waited patiently outside of that edifice until allowed inside once again to view the miraculous improvements bestowed upon them by their leaders.

But this time things have changed. There is a pessimism haunting this society and it is not going away: the belief, held deep-down, that the time-honored structure of the Meiji state has seen its better days; that a new national ethos and a new source of collective pride must be found and nurtured.

This is the transition to the next phase of Japanese social life. The side effects of this transition are apathy and hopelessness. Yet the Japanese people are gradually coming to realize that it is they themselves who must take responsibility for the misdirection of the past decade, that their dedication to their own personal welfare has now become the sole route to social betterment.

Not a minute goes by in Japan without someone in the media blaming politicians and bureaucrats for the unprecedented floundering and waste that

---

[(p.70)24]　**shrivel**　しなびる，しぼむ，しおれる．
[2]　**shoddy**　まがいものの，粗雑な；不正な．
[2]　**airbrush**　エアブラシで修整する[吹き付ける]．
[16]　**edifice**　（宮殿・教会など堂々とした）建物．
[23]　**apathy**　無感動；無関心，冷淡，しらけ．
[28]　**unprecedented**　先例[前例]のない，空前の，前代未聞の．

plague Japanese life today. But the Japanese people have themselves been the most skilled masters at evading personal responsibility for any action that might touch their lives.

I am convinced that the Japan that you will see in the coming decades will be fundamentally different from the Japan of the 20th century. And it will come about through the realization by the Japanese people that, for better or worse, they have no one to blame for their fate but themselves. [5]

[(p.71)28]　**flounder**　もがく，あがく，のたうつ；もたつく．
[1]　　　　**plague**　疫病[災いなど]にかからせる，悩ませる，苦しめる．

Questions

1. What does the author mean by "communal aggrandizement" on page 68, line 9?

(A) all people demanding their share of the common wealth
(B) each person becoming wealthy for the sake of all
(C) all people considering their welfare in common
(D) each person feeling pride in his or her own achievements

2. According to the author, what was the major goal of the Japanese of the Meiji Era?

(A) to colonize Korea and China
(B) to catch up with and overtake the West
(C) to create a democracy like those in the West
(D) to educate all Japanese citizens in foreign languages

3. What does the author mean by "the Kaiser's club" on page 69, line 4?

(A) the colonial powers
(B) seeing Japan as part of Asia
(C) having cynical and sinister aims
(D) modeling Japanese society on Germany's

4. According to the author, Japan enjoyed the proverbial bubble economy. What did NOT happen during this time?

(A) Japanese were buying a lot of major overseas assets.
(B) A Japanese publisher bought a major British publishing house.
(C) A senior planner in the Japanese government devised a plan for Japan to buy the state of Montana.
(D) The price of land in the Tokyo metropolitan area came to be worth more than California.

5. **Choose the word below that is dissimilar in meaning to the word "inflated" on page 70, line 15.**

(A) inexpensive
(B) exorbitant
(C) costly
(D) extravagant

6. **Why does the author, on page 70, line 20, see the image of the bubble as a con?**

(A) because it did not provide benefit consistently to society
(B) because when it burst, it burst evenly throughout the society
(C) because much of the consumption then was really degradation and rot
(D) because it concentrated on corporate, not personal, areas

7. **The phrase "digging in their heels" on page 71, line 13, is closest in meaning to**

(A) deferring to the opinions of others
(B) marching forward persistently
(C) giving in when necessary
(D) persisting in their opinions

8. **Choose the most appropriate title for this article from those below.**

(A) Apathy and Hopeless in Japan Yesterday and Today
(B) Politicians and Bureaucrats are to Blame for Japan's Problems
(C) The 1980s: the ideal state and how to return to it
(D) The Future of Japan Depends on Japanese People Taking Responsibility for their Lives

You will hear the entire text of "Where do the Japanese stand today?" Immediately following the text, you will hear Questions 9 and 10.
Listen carefully to the text and questions, and write your answers in the space provided below.

9. _____

10. _____

New horizons beckon as Train Man heads nowhere fast

Roger Pulvers

introduction

いつの時代も社会はみずからそれぞれの在り方を定義する。
これは 2005 年の 7 月 10 日付の *The Japan Times* の連載コラム Counterpoint に寄稿したものであるが、ここで指摘するように、ぼくが日本にたどり着いた 1967 年頃に日本人と聞いてまず連想されるイメージは何かと言えば、あるいは当時彼らが何にたとえられたかと言えば、「戦うサラリーマン」（the battling salaryman）であった。このホワイトカラーの労働者の意味を示す salaryman は、元々和製英語だったが、今では英語圏でかなりよく用いられる。

salaryman は今も変わらず日本人を象徴するものとしてもちろん健在ではあるが、しかし、その一位の座はいつの間にかちょっと気味が悪い「オタク」たちに奪われてしまったようだ。しかし、この新しい日本人の象徴もやはり同じようにそのうちにどこかに追いやられてしまって、また別のタイプの人が新しい日本人のイメージとして出てくることだろう。それがどんなタイプの人になるかは、皆それぞれ意見が異なるだろうが。

しかし、社会においてどんなものが流行し、人々が何に熱狂しようとも、日本のような複雑でいろんな要素を持ち合わせた国が、たった一人の人間によって象徴される、というようなことはまずありえないと思う。

The Japanese nation seems to be firmly in the grip of the otaku.

Every society seeks an overriding metaphor that is emblematic of a particular decade or era. Well, the metaphor of the moment in this country is the lifestyle and communication style (or, noncommunication style) of the otaku.

The otaku novel *Densha Otoko* (*Train Man*) grew out of an internet [5] bulletin board on Channel 2, and has sold over a million copies and been made into a feature film and a TV drama since it was published last October by Shinchosha.

This feckless "classic of the chat room" depicts the life, if you can call it that, of a full-on otaku who has about as much chance of getting a girl as [10] Woody Allen in a Ukrainian convent. But thanks to a display of artless altruism toward a stressed-out damsel on a train, charm oozes out of his googly-eyed, two-left-feet, klutzy presence.

Now, Japan is the fad society to end all fad societies, and when something takes off here it spreads like wildfire. A train pulls into the station and someone who is respected hollers, "Everybody off! We've gotta take another train!" — and sure enough, people file out of the carriage without complaint and march across the platform to the next departing train. It's the new direction for everyone: They may not know where the train is going, but it's a novel turn of events that everyone else is taking, too, and they all seem content. This is the metaphor of the train that represents Fad Japan, and in 2005 the Train Man is calling the stations. [5]

What exactly is an otaku? [10]

The word itself is an honorific, formal and now obsolescent form of "you." The gawky nerdy goofballs who are more at home breathing on their computers and Game Boys than on members of the opposite sex were said to use this stiff term when trying to approach women. Their use of "otaku" for "you" in, say, the expression Otaku wa ikaga desu ka? (How about you?) is equivalent to a fellow trying to strike up a conversation in English with, "What may I do for you, Miss?" — likely adding for dorky good measure such seductive lines as, "What's a nice girl like you doing in a place like this?" or "Do you come here often, Miss? I know I do." [15]

That such a nebbish would have anything but a long string of lonely nights before him is hardly surprising. [20]

[(p.75)10]　**full-on**　まったくの，もろの．

[(p.75)10–11]　**... as Woody Allen in a Ukrainian convent**　要するに，「ユダヤ人俳優のウディ・アレンがウクライナの女子修道院で女の子をナンパするのはほとんどありえないことだが，超オタクな男性は，それと同じぐらい女の子と付き合う機会に恵まれない」ということ．

[(p.75)11]　**altruism**　利他［愛他］主義（⇔ egoism）．

[(p.75)12]　**ooze**　（液体・湿気などが）しみ［にじみ］出る．

[1]　**klutzy**　不器用な，ぶざまな，うすのろの．

[12]　**honorific**　敬称，敬語．

[12]　**obsolescent**　すたれかかった．

[13]　**gawky**　（体ばかり大きくて）ぎこちない，ぶざまな．

[13]　**goofball**　まぬけ，どじ．

[18]　**seductive**　誘惑［魅惑］的な，人を引きつける．

[21]　**nebbish**　無能で意気地なし［人］．

The otaku culture takes artistic expression in a number of ways: addiction to anime and manga, particularly the cuter end of the genres; being hooked on electronic goods; worshipping adorable idols. In this world, Hello Kitty is not just a Japanese Mickey Mouse substitute, she is the Guardian Angel of inner feelings: a lovable smooth-plastic cat that serves as the only constant sweetie-puss.

The otaku freaks out over those things in the subculture that society finds vaguely weird as obsessions.

A person who is crazy about stamps or steam trains may be a maniac, in the Japanese terminology; but they are never otaku. Stamps and trains are acceptable obsessions. The dyed-in-the-wool otaku is different. He spends his every available moment in Tokyo's "Electric Town" of Akihabara surrounded by his beloved gadgets, his fantasy-stirring comics and his cutesy figurines — to whom he relates more readily than he does to fellow human beings.

As such, the otaku is essentially narcissistic. Theirs is a "virtual masturbation" culture focused on fantasy objects and images.

So how did this otaku type become the working metaphor of an entire culture?

Look at the metaphor of the previous generation of Japanese, the Battling Salaryman, called a modern samurai replacing sword with briefcase. The best-selling study "Tateshakai no ningen kankei (Human Relations in Japan)," published in 1967 by Tokyo University Prof. Chie Nakane, set the tone for this type. Japanese society was described as a vertical society in which people knew their station and responded to others on the basis of it.

The engine of Japanese power in the 1960s and '70s was the salaryman who gave his all to the company (read country) at the expense of family. His loyalties were above him.

But the 1990s brought recession and the loss of social momentum. No

---

[3] **adorable** 可愛い.
[5–6] **sweetie-puss** 可愛い猫ちゃん.
[11] **dyed-in-the-wool** 徹底した，根っからの.
[15] **narcissistic** 自己陶酔的な.

longer was the intrepid salaryman the working metaphor of a nation. According to a recent government report, only 16 percent of young people think their parents' lives are worth living for themselves. Behind this, there seems to be a loss of faith among the young in the hard-working company man — he who used to be called in the United States "the man in the gray flannel suit." [5]

Where can young people turn? During their time of disillusion with the postwar work ethic, American young people looked to the beatniks and the hippies for inspiration. The young generation of America in the tumultuous 1965–75 decade chose to follow the lead of long hair, passionate protest and opting out of what they saw as the stifling and drudging "system." [10]

With no war here to protest — as there was in Vietnam back then for American youth (and many of their contemporaries beyond those shores, as well) — and given the typical Japanese apathy that pervades all generations regarding social and political movements, where could the young Japanese of the 1990s turn? The answer is, they turned to fantasy; to escape. At least the otaku is [15] harmless, they might say. A guy who is into gadgets, animated characters and dolls doesn't have the power to hurt others.

I don't think that this metaphor for Japanese society will last much longer. No one is going to entrust their future to the Train Man. He represents a culture that, if curiously attractive and creative, is heading nowhere fast. [20]

The otaku culture certainly represents a dumbing down of Japan; and when the Japanese dumb down, they dumb down methodically and thoroughly. The culture of ideas and of intellectual polemics that once held sway here is right now exceedingly dormant; and the models of dynamic progress that are evident in other countries in Asia are in Japanese pieces. [25]

What will the new metaphor of Japan be once the next train pulls into the station?

---

[8] **tumultuous** 騒がしい，騒々しい，荒々しい，荒れ狂う．
[10] **drudging** 単調な，飽きあきする．
[21, 22] **dumb down** 知的水準が下がる．
[22] **methodically** 整然と，系統的に．
[24] **dormant** （人などが）眠っている（ような）；睡眠状態の；機能・知能・感情などが休止状態にある．

It is sad to say that all of the working metaphors for this country have been male dominated. However, the Foreign Ministry reported that as of Oct. 1, 2004, the number of Japanese people living and working overseas was 961,307–467,627 of them men, but with women in the majority, at 493,680. Wouldn't it be nice if this outward-looking, international Japanese woman — in whatever form the culture chose to portray her — became the new symbol of Japan? [5]

Once thing is for sure: no one would then be apt to say, "Nerds have all the luck."

---

[2]   **dominate** （…を）支配する，圧する，威圧する；（…に）優位を占める．
[7]   **nerd** ばか，ぐず，遅れてる[やぼったい，ダサい]やつ，(社会性がなく趣味・研究にのめり込んだ)専門ばか，おたく，ガリ勉屋．形容詞は nerdy.

Questions

1. According to the article, how many copies of *Densha Otoko* have sold?

(A) up to 1,000,000 copies
(B) more than 1,000,000 copies
(C) more than 10,000,000 copies
(D) not exceeding 1,000,000 copies

2. What does the author mean by "a fad society to end all fad societies" on page 76, line 2?

(A) a fad society that is sure to come to an end
(B) a society in which fads are relatively important
(C) a society in which riding on trains is an enjoyable fad
(D) the ultimate fad society

3. What does the author mean by "hardly surprising" on page 76, line 22?

(A) just a bit surprising
(B) not very surprising
(C) somewhat surprising
(D) totally surprising

4. The word "gadgets" on page 77, line 13, is closest in meaning to

(A) periodicals
(B) fashionable clothes
(C) gimmicks
(D) trips abroad

5. What does the term "his loyalties were above him" on page 77, lines 26–27, mean?

(A) He thought of his company before himself.
(B) He thought of his family before himself.
(C) He saw himself as the engine of Japanese power in the 1960s and '70s.
(D) He paid expenses for his family from his salary at the company.

6 The word "intrepid" on page 78, line 1, can NOT be changed to

(A) villainous
(B) heroic
(C) brave
(D) courageous

7. According to a Foreign Ministry report in 2004, is it men or women who comprise the majority of Japanese living and working overseas?

(A) women
(B) men
(C) the number is the same
(D) exact figures are not yet available

8. Why does the author think that the metaphor of the otaku won't last?

(A) because people are only curious about its attractiveness and creativity
(B) because the culture of ideas and polemics is about to come back
(C) because other Asian countries have experienced something similar but eventually rejected it
(D) because it has no set destination

You will hear the entire text of "New horizons beckon as Train Man heads nowhere fast." Immediately following the text, you will hear Questions 9 and 10. Listen carefully to the text and questions, and write your answers in the space provided below.

9. _____

10. _____

The stage is set for genuine change

Roger Pulvers

introduction

明治時代の日本が直面した大きな問題は、ほぼ欧米諸国が掌握する世界において、その足場をいかにして築くか、ということであった。それに対して21世紀の日本が直面している問題は、アジア諸国との関係をいかに築くか、ということになるだろう。

この記事は元々 The Japan Times に5年以上前に寄稿したものだが、ここで提起した問題は、今も変わらず論じられている。すなわち、日本は、戦時中にアジア諸国に対して何をしたか、特に中国や韓国と朝鮮に対して何をしたか、正式に認めなければならない、ということである。

ぼく自身は日本国民の大半はそれを甘んじて受け入れる用意があると思う。しかし、政府内の権力者たちが、国民にそれをさせずにいるのではないだろうか。

アジア環太平洋地域における協調関係をさらに発展させるには、過去にしたことを日本国民が世界に対して正直に報告するしかないと思う。まさに今こそ、公式の日本史を、事実を捻じ曲げず、ありのままに報告すべきだ。

When I first arrived in Japan in 1967, the Japanese were in the throes of an obsession. This was an obsession with change. The Japanese economy was about to be confirmed as the world's second largest. New models of cars and appliances were greeted by the populace with a craving interest. Japanese businessmen returning from stints overseas were implored by their compatriots to comment on the upgraded affluence that had overtaken the country in their absence. [5]

A Japanese journalist eagerly asked me just such a question in my early days here. "Japan has really changed, hasn't it?"

"I don't know," I said. "I just got here." [10]

As we look back on those years of heady, incessant growth — the years that formed what came to be known as the Japanese miracle — and their promise of a good and fair deal for all Japanese, we can now see clearly where the train of state slipped the track: The postwar Japanese excelled at growth for its own sake, but were stymied by the requirements for the uses of that growth. [15]

The stage is set for genuine change

The embarrassing dilemma of possessing riches and managing them poorly, however, was no mere accident of incompetence. To call Japan's leaders incompetent merely begs the questions of cause and intent. The fact is that the Japanese people, with the encouragement and blessing of their postwar American mentors, gave the ownership, planning and operation of the vehicles of [5] power to a class of managers who were steeped in the nationalistic ethics of prewar Japan.

These managers — the mainstream politicians of the country since the mid-'50s — had not absorbed the lessons of democracy that presumably formed the basis of the new Japanese morality. And it was not in the commercial [10] interests of the United States (are there any other interests that the U.S. authentically recognizes?) for Japan to be truly democratic either . . . nor is it now. A democratic Japan would be a progressive and less easily manipulated Japan.

As the world moved into the 21st century, there were two dominant burdens that Japan carried with it from the dying century. One was the legacy of Japan's [15] war in Asia and the concomitant responsibility of Emperor Showa in its complicity; the other, the oppressive social and political ethos that Japan's leaders have used, under the astute bluff of a seemingly democratic rhetoric, to control society.

In 2000, then-Prime Minister Yoshiro Mori went on record for making what [20] some called gaffes, dropping obtuse and anachronistic clangers here and there, that Japan is a divine country and that it has the emperor at its core. This so-

---

[(p.82)1]   **in the throes of ...**   （問題・困難など）と必死に取り組んで，...と（悪戦）苦闘して．
[(p.82)4]   **appliance**   （特に家庭用の）器具；装置，設備；電気製品［器具］．
[(p.82)5]   **stint**   （一定の量の）割り当てられた仕事，一定期間の仕事［勤務］，勤め；勤務期間．
[(p.82)11] **incessant**   絶え間ない，間断のない，ひっきりなしの．
[(p.82)15] **stymie** (*or* **stymy**)   （...を）挫折させる，困った立場に追い込む．発音にも注意（/stáimi/）．
[2]   **incompetence**   無能力；不適格；無資格．
[16]   **concomitant**   付随する，伴う，同時にある［起こる］．
[18]   **bluff**   虚勢，こけおどし；からいばり，はったり．
[21]   **gaffe**   失言，失態．
[21]   **obtuse**   （刃・角の）鈍い，とがっていない；鈍感な，愚鈍な；はっきりとは感じない（痛みなど）；わかりにくい，不明瞭な（ことば）．
[21]   **anachronistic**   時代錯誤の．

called gaffe caused a stir in the media but, needless to say, did not lead to his ouster.

In the autumn of 1995, the head of the Management and Coordination Agency, Takami Eto, was obliged to resign over his remarks in guarded praise of the brutal Japanese occupation of Korea between 1910 and 1945. Eto said that Japan had done "some good things" in Korea.

In May 1994 the atrocity at Nanking was debunked by a former interior minister as being a "trumped up" event. In fact, over the past 45 years similar statements by Japanese leaders using what should be the restricted terminology of Japanese imperialism and ethnic superiority attest to the fact that the elite class of politicians in power are, deep down, unreconstructed nationalists of the old hellfire persuasion.

The use by public officials of such words as "kokutai" (national polity) and "sangokujin" (alien) may seem harmless enough. But in reality these words are potent reminders of a most offensive nationalism. They are emblems on the banners of the leaders who brandish them, emblems that remind us all that their ability to flaunt these symbols of reaction before our very eyes can, at their whim, be the forewarning of a thoroughgoing suppression.

So the prolonged and constant suppression of the truth and the secrecy over Japan's past deeds have been no accidental flaw in an otherwise open society. Make no mistake. These have served the interests of the men who derailed the train of democracy for their own greater good, as well as for the good of their patrons, clients and numerous sycophants. It has been crucial for them to keep Japanese people in the dark about what was done during the war. Were the truth to come out and be recognized by a wide public here, the entire leadership of

---

[1]　**stir**　かき回すこと，かき混ぜ；動かすこと；そよぎ．この場合は，a stir で，「(世間の)騒ぎ」．

[8]　**a "trumped up" event**　でっちあげの出来事，捏造(ねつぞう)した出来事．trumped-up (でっちあげた，捏造した)と普通はハイフンが入るが，ここではクォテーションに囲まれているのでこう表記．

[10]　**attest to**　(物事が)(...の)証拠となる；(人が)(...を)証明する．

[15]　**emblem**　象徴，表象．

[16]　**brandish**　(刀などを)(脅すように，得意そうに)振り回す，打ち振る．

[17]　**flaunt**　見せびらかす．

[(p.85)2]　**delegitimize**　非合法化する，...の権威(法的地位)を失墜させる．

[(p.85)4]　**with pieces of the pie**　piece of... は「...の一部，自分の力の一部」，pie は「全体，総額」．

this country, the leadership that has ruled over the past half century, would be readily delegitimized and thrown out of power.

The design was to focus a timid and industrious populace on the benefits of constant growth, to buy their loyalty with pieces of the pie. But the paint of the design's slogan "you've never had it so good" began to chip off in the early [5] '90s, until now, when the message itself is barely readable.

This is why the powers-that-be in Japan fear this particular recessive economic era the most. The Japanese people are admirably stoic and will take almost anything. But they want to be taken seriously. They are coming to realize gradually that the forfeiture of the integrity of their history for material [10] gain may not be such a sanguine tradeoff in the new century.

And this brings us to the question of the war responsibility of Emperor Showa. I have no doubt but that the Japanese people will come to terms with Emperor Showa's obvious role in the major policy decisions of the '30s and '40s. The only impediment to this has been, and continues to be, the stake that [15] the leadership of this country has had in its sly obfuscation.

When the truth about Japan's actions in Asia during the war and the role played by the postwar rulers in its withholding come out, the trauma of revelation, I believe, will not be as severe as some people reckon. To the contrary, the process of revealing it will be not only tolerable but liberating. [20]

The stage is set for another era of continual change, this time not of a materialistic but of an ethical and political nature.

I cannot help but feel that the coming decade will set the stage for liberal-minded and genuinely democratic young Japanese to step up and make their mark. All the props are at their disposal and they have only to write their lines. [25]

[10] **forfeiture** （財産の）没収；（名声・権利などの）喪失.
[11] **sanguine** （気質など）陽気な，自信のある．この場合は，「楽観的な，よい結果が望める」．
[16] **obfuscation** （心などを）暗くすること；（判断などを）曇らせること；（問題などを）不明瞭にすること，わかりにくくすること．
[25] **prop** 「支柱；支え，頼り；支えとなる人」の意味もあるが，ここでは「（舞台の）小道具」の意味もかけている．
[25] **(be) at [in] sb's disposal** 人の自由になる，勝手に使える．"This money is at your disposal." で，「この金は自由に使いなさい」となる．例 "Please come to my office at any time," said Prof. Watkins. "I am at your disposal."（「ぼくの研究室にいつでも来てください」とワトキンズ教授は言った．「いつでも相談に乗ります」）

JAPAN

Questions

1. What does the author mean by "no mere accident of incompetence" on page 83, line 2?

   (A) that the postwar leaders were not mean, but just made a lot of mistakes
   (B) that the postwar leaders loved Japan and their mistakes are understandable because of this love
   (C) that the postwar leaders had to beg Americans for help and that caused their dilemma
   (D) that the postwar leaders deliberately planned the economy that way

2. The word "astute" on page 83, line 18, is closest in meaning to

   (A) absurd
   (B) reserved
   (C) shrewd
   (D) grateful

3. Which of the below words is dissimilar in meaning to the word "flaw" on page 84, line 20?

   (A) blemish
   (B) advantage
   (C) defect
   (D) fault

4. What does "pieces of the pie" on page 85, line 4, mean?

   (A) money
   (B) better food
   (C) a new job
   (D) making Japan economically strong again

5. What does the author see as preventing a full disclosure of Emperor Showa's war responsibility?

(A) If it were disclosed, today's leaders might lose power.
(B) If it were disclosed, the leaders would be able to obfuscate the reasons.
(C) If it were disclosed, the Japanese people would not believe it entirely.
(D) If it were disclosed, today's leaders would accept the result.

6. "I cannot help but feel" on page 85, line 23, means

(A) I do not particularly feel
(B) Nothing can help me feel
(C) I am obliged to feel
(D) I need no help to feel

7. The phrase "make their mark" on page 85, lines 24–25, is closest in meaning to

(A) make the same mistakes as the previous generation
(B) diligently prevent wars whenever possible
(C) make sure that Japan is never bullied by foreign countries
(D) personally make a difference to Japanese life

8. The phrase "write their lines" on page 85, line 25, is closest in meaning to

(A) study literature and become literary critics
(B) draw the outline of plans for the city of the future
(C) write emails to their friends and tell them what is in their heart
(D) decide on what they want to do and proceed with it

You will hear the entire text of "The stage is set for genuine change." Immediately following the text, you will hear Questions 9 and 10.
Listen carefully to the text and questions, and write your answers in the space provided below.

9. _____

10. _____

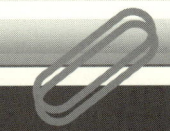

SCIENCE AND TECHNOLOGY

Sick with worry

Jerome Groopman

> **Introduction**
>
> Jerome Groopman 博士のこの論文 "Sick with worry" は、*New Yorker* 誌の 2003 年 8 月 11 日号に掲載された。グループマン博士は、この記事のなかで、社会問題となっている心気症（憂鬱症、ヒポコンドリー）を取り上げている。肉体的に悪い部分が確認できない病気を、ぼくらはすべて「精神病」（psychosomatic diseases）として片付けてしまっているかもしれない。それは、気の持ち方次第でなんとかなるもの、ぐらいに考えてしまっているかもしれない。("Sick with worry" は、「病気になるぐらいとても心配して」という意味である。92 ページの注も参照のこと。)
>
> 　しかし、こうした病気に悩まされている人たちにすれば、事態は深刻である。からだのどこかを怪我したり、脳細胞に問題が生じれば、痛みを感じる。その痛みは実際の痛みなのか、それとも想像上の痛みなのか、誰が特定できるだろう？
>
> 　科学や医学の問題を文章で論じる書き手はほかにもいるが、グループマン博士は極めて明快に、読者をうまく引き寄せながら、論を進める。さらにグループマン博士は医師の役割について常に疑問を挟みつつ、その一方で患者の気持ちを理解しながら、やさしく彼らを見つめる。博士が患者の知性と感性を軽んじることは決してない。
>
> 　その昔、医者はまさに神のような存在で、絶対に間違いのない処方箋と、高価な薬を患者に与えてくれる、と信じられていた。医師がミスを犯したかもしれない、彼らに問題があるかもしれない、と疑われることは決してなかった。
>
> 　グループマン博士は、常に患者の視点から、人道的に判断しようとする。日本における医師と患者の関係についても、博士はたくさんのことを教えてくれる。

Amanda was sure that she had contracted leukemia, developed a brain tumor, and had a stroke — all around the same time. She made this self-diagnosis while experiencing intermittent discomfort in her abdomen and feeling a persistent wooziness in her head. She often felt off balance, as if she were walking on a warped floor. "I was also really worried about my spleen," [5] she told me in a recent conversation. (Amanda is not her real name.) For almost a year, she had sought explanations for her various complaints, discussing her symptoms with twenty physicians in her H.M.O. All of them told her that they could find nothing wrong. These doctors spent little time with her, and none offered a follow-up appointment, although they readily referred her to [10] other physicians.

    With growing frustration, Amanda visited more specialists, undergoing physical examinations, blood tests, and sonograms. Nothing abnormal was found, but with each test she became more convinced that she was seriously ill. She kept looking for a doctor who would tell her, unequivocally, that her symptoms could not possibly indicate a fatal sickness. When doctors couldn't give her absolute assurance, she concluded that something terrible must be wrong with her. I asked Amanda, a petite woman with a lightly freckled face, why she thought doctors kept referring her to others. She was perplexed by the question. "We live in a litigious society," she said. "Maybe they were afraid of lawsuits, if they missed something." She paused. "Maybe they were confused by what was wrong with me."

    Amanda, who is thirty-three years old and teaches theatre arts at a West Coast college, has suffered from medical anxieties many times before. Several years ago, she was in a travelling theatrical group for children, and played a role that required her to wear an elephant costume for more than a hundred days in a row. After a long day spent in rehearsal and onstage, she often felt exhausted and queasy. Most people would attribute these feelings to stress, but she was convinced that her symptoms indicated a dire disease; one day, during

---

- [(p.90)1] **contract** （病気・ウイルスに）かかる，感染する．
- [(p.90)1] **leukemia** 白血病．
- [(p.90)3] **self-diagnosis** 自己診断．
- [(p.90)4] **wooziness** woozy (頭のぼんやりした，混乱した，気分のすぐれない，くらくら［むかむか］した)の名詞形．
- [(p.90)5] **spleen** 脾(ひ)，脾臓．
- [(p.90)8] **H.M.O.** (= health maintenance organization) 保険維持機構．希望して加入した個人・家族に対してメンバーの医師が包括的な医療を行なう組織．資金はあらかじめ定められた医療費を定期的に支払うことによって賄う．HMOと略すこともある．
- [3] **sonogram** 超音波検査図．
- [5] **unequivocally** あいまいでなく，紛らわしくなく；明白に，率直に．
- [9] **perplex** (人を)困らせる，当惑させる．
- [10] **litigious** 訴訟好きな；論争好きな；訴訟できる［すべき］；訴訟(上)の．
- [18] **queasy** 吐き気がする；むかむかする．

a prolonged episode of abdominal pain, she thought she might be dying and, in a panic, asked a colleague to take her to a local hospital. The doctors there failed to detect anything out of order. The next night, she went again, and once more the E.R. physicians sent her home.

Amanda's fears about illness began when she was nine, after she heard that a schoolmate had almost died from a severe case of chicken pox. As a teenager, she was terrified each time she had to visit a doctor. "I remember when I was fourteen years old, and I was sitting in biology class and had a doctor's appointment later that day," she said. "I was so scared, I couldn't think." She entered college at the peak of the AIDS epidemic. Though she told me that she "wasn't strongly at risk for H.I.V." — she had few sexual partners and regularly used protection — she became consumed by the idea that she was infected. "I really thought I had the virus," she said. Shortly after graduation, Amanda moved to New York City, where she got a job in a bookstore. "Each day, I checked reference books in the store, and called people about AIDS," she said. "It got so bad that my co-workers tried to keep me away from the health section."

People like Amanda populate every doctor's waiting room. Studies show that at least a quarter of all patients report symptoms that appear to have no physical basis, and that one in ten continues to believe that he has a terminal disease even after the doctor has found him to be healthy. Experts say that between three and six per cent of patients seen by primary-care physicians suffer from hypochondria, the irrational fear of illness. The number is likely growing, thanks to increased medical reporting in the media, which devotes particular attention to scary new diseases like SARS, and to the internet, which provides a wealth of clinical information (and misinformation) that can help turn a concerned patient into a neurotic one. Nevertheless, hypochondria is rarely discussed in the doctor's office. The "worried well," as sufferers are sometimes called, typically feel insulted by any suggestion that their symp-

---

[3]　**detect**　（病気などを）見つける，発見する．
[27]　**neurotic**　神経の；神経症の．
[28]　**The "worried well"**　元気だけどよく心配する人たち．worried sick (= sick with worry「(…のことで)(病気になるほど)とても心配して」にかけた言い方．

toms have a psychological basis. Most patients are given a formal diagnosis of hypochondria only after ten or so years of seeing physicians, if they get such a diagnosis at all.

Doctors often dislike their hypochondriac patients; they consume inordinate amounts of time, and strain hospital resources with their interminable complaints. In the United States, it is estimated, twenty billion dollars a year is spent on patients whose psychological distress requires repeated tests and procedures. Many doctors and nurses make fun of hypochondriacs, calling them "crocks" and "turkeys." The favored epithet among interns and residents is GOMER, which stands for Get Out of My Emergency Room. Many doctors are relieved when a hypochondriac leaves them for another physician.

Hypochondria is so hazily understood that most doctors have no clear idea how to manage patients who suffer from it. The disorder is particularly tricky for the primary-care physician, who often sees patients with nebulous complaints and must judge how deeply to explore these ambiguous symptoms. The doctor knows that a fair number of people in his waiting room each day will prove to have no physical disorder — yet he must remain open to the possibility that each patient might truly be sick. Hypochondriacs, in effect, risk deafening a physician with their relentless background noise.

I am a medical specialist who cares for patients with blood diseases, cancer, and AIDS. Several years ago, I was a consulting oncologist for a woman who had developed breast cancer. The tumor had been found early and was removed by surgery. I saw her only once or twice a year, but her internist had told me that she was a severe hypochondriac. At each visit, she unloaded a series of complaints, but almost always mentioned having a queasy feeling in her stomach. Her husband sometimes accompanied her to my office; once, when I asked her how long she had suffered from the stomach symptom, he interrupted and said, "Since I married her." The couple had been together for thirty years. I looked at him from the corner of my eye and we exchanged a dismissive look. Some weeks later, I was called by the patient's primary-care doctor, who told me that she had almost died from sepsis owing to an infected gall-

---

[9]　**epithet**　あだ名, 通り名; 軽蔑の言葉, 悪口.
[31]　**sepsis**　敗血症. 複数形は sepses.

SCIENCE AND TECHNOLOGY

bladder. I was distraught that I had treated her complaints with such a cavalier attitude. Sometimes, even a hypochondriac's complaints are valid.

Another reason that doctors are uncomfortable with hypochondriacs is that physicians routinely become afflicted with the disorder themselves. After all, doctors are trained to be exquisite observers of subtle symptoms. As one colleague put it, "When we learned about Hodgkin's disease in medical school, everyone was feeling his lymph nodes, and for several weeks was terrified that he was on the brink of being diagnosed."

This winter, I injured my right hand, and it was not clear whether one of the small bones in my wrist was fractured. An orthopedic surgeon suggested a bone scan. The night after the scan, he called me at home. "It doesn't look like a fracture," he said. "Before we deal with the wrist, however, we need to evaluate the suspicious areas in your left upper ribs." One radiologist thought that the scan, which had surveyed my entire body, showed changes in the ribs which were consistent with metastatic cancer.

As I hung up the phone, my hand trembling, I noticed that my left upper ribs ached. They hadn't hurt before the call. My wife, who is also a doctor, was out of town. I reached her on the phone, and she tried to reassure me that bone scans are notoriously inaccurate and are often misread. I was unable to sleep that night, and the pain in my left ribs became more intense. At eight o'clock the next morning, I was the first in line at the radiology department to have further X-rays done. My ribs were normal. But the discomfort didn't subside for a week, and it was nearly two weeks before I could fully dismiss the fear that I was going to die from bone cancer.

[(p.93)31–1] **gallbladder**　胆嚢(たんのう).

[1]　**cavalier**　傲慢な，尊大な.

[6]　**Hodgkin's disease**　ホジキン病(悪性リンパ腫).

[7]　**lymph node**　リンパ節［腺］.

[8]　**on the brink of**　今にも．．．しようとして，．．．の瀬戸際に．例 Those two countries are on the brink of war. War could break out at any time. (あの二つの国のあいだでは今にも戦争が起こりそうな状態だ．ほんとうにいつ起きても不思議ではない．)

[8]　**diagnose**　（．．．を）（．．．と）診断する.

[10]　**orthopedic**　整形外科の.

[13]　**radiologist**　放射［X］線学者；放射線医師；レントゲン技師.

[15]　**metastatic**　転移性の.

Sick with worry

Questions

1. The sentence "She was perplexed by the question." on page 91, lines 9–10, can be changed to

(A) She was delighted with the question.
(B) She was angered by the question.
(C) She was puzzled by the question.
(D) She was enthusiastic about the question.

2. What question was Amanda perplexed by?

(A) why her doctors referred her to other doctors
(B) why her doctors kept missing something in their diagnoses
(C) why her doctors were confused about her condition
(D) why Dr. Groopman asked her the question in the first place

3. The word "abdominal" on page 92, line 1, refers to the

(A) stomach
(B) head
(C) spine
(D) arms and legs

4. What does "consumed by the idea" of infection on page 92, line 12, mean?

(A) She purchased any medicine that made her feel better.
(B) She ate foods that stopped the infection.
(C) She was pretty certain that her virus wasn't AIDS.
(D) She was overtaken by the idea of infection.

5. What does the author mean by "Hypochondriacs . . . risk deafening a physician with their relentless background noise." on page 93, lines 18–19?

(A) Hypochondriacs run the risk of becoming deaf from their imagined illnesses.
(B) Hypochondriacs talk so much about their illnesses that doctors can barely hear what they say.
(C) Doctors try to listen hard to hypochondriacs, even though it is often risky to do so.
(D) Doctors lack background in dealing with hypochondriacs and their problems.

SCIENCE AND TECHNOLOGY

6. The word "nebulous" on page 93, line 14, is closest in meaning to

(A) exact
(B) precise
(C) vague
(D) magnificent

7. The word "distraught" on page 94, line 1, is closest in meaning to

(A) upset
(B) calm
(C) perceptive
(D) considerate

8. Dr. Groopman felt intense pain in his left ribs because

(A) his radiologist told him that he had cancer in his ribs
(B) his wife told him that the radiologist had misread his scan
(C) his inability to sleep caused the pain to increase
(D) he was virtually convinced that he had bone cancer

You will hear the entire text of "Sick with worry." Immediately following the text, you will hear Questions 9 and 10.
Listen carefully to the text and questions, and write your answers in the space provided below.

9. _____

10. _____

Climate change: instant expert

Fred Pearce

> **introduction**
>
> これは *New Scientist* の 2004 年 12 月 13 日号に掲載された記事である。著者 Fred Pearce は、どこかの政治家が言うようなことではあるが、今日の地球温暖化の問題に警鐘を鳴らす。特に先進国の国民は、エネルギーの効果的な使い方を講じなければならない... それも今すぐ。
>
> 　日本やアメリカのような国の政府こそ、地球温暖化を防ぐエネルギーの使い方を推奨しなければならないのに、日常生活において温暖化の原因となるエネルギーを一体どこにどうやって廃棄したらいいかについては、個人一人ひとりにまかされているのが実情だ。
>
> 　マーク・トウェインはかつて言った、「誰もが天気についてあれこれ言うが、誰もそれについて何かしようとはしない」(Everybody talks about the weather, but nobody does anything about it) と。
>
> 　だから、今こそ何かを変えられるチャンスなのだ...個人が何かを変えることができるのだから。

Climate change is with us. A decade ago, it was conjecture. Now the future is unfolding before our eyes. Canada's Inuit see it in disappearing Arctic ice and permafrost. The shantytown dwellers of Latin America and Southern Asia see it in lethal storms and floods. Europeans see it in disappearing glaciers, forest fires and fatal heat waves. [5]

Scientists see it in tree rings, ancient coral and bubbles trapped in ice cores. These reveal that the world has not been as warm as it is now for a millennium or more. The three warmest years on record have all occurred since 1998; 19 of the warmest 20 since 1980. And Earth has probably never warmed as fast as in the past 30 years — a period when natural influences on global temperatures, [10] such as solar cycles and volcanoes should have cooled us down.

Climatologists reporting for the UN Intergovernmental Panel on Climate Change (IPCC) say we are seeing global warming caused by human activities.

Global greenhouse [15]

People are causing the change by burning nature's vast stores of coal, oil and natural gas. This releases billions of tonnes of carbon dioxide (CO2) every year, although the changes may actually have started with the dawn of agriculture, say some scientists.

The physics of the "greenhouse effect" has been a matter of scientific fact for a century. CO2 is a greenhouse gas that traps the Sun's radiation within the troposphere, the lower atmosphere. It has accumulated along with other man-made greenhouse gases, such as methane and chlorofluorocarbons (CFCs). Some studies suggest that cosmic rays may also be involved in warming. [5]

If current trends continue, we will raise atmospheric CO2 concentrations to double pre-industrial levels during this century. That will probably be enough to raise global temperatures by around 2°C to 5°C. Some warming is certain, but the degree will be determined by cycles involving melting ice, the oceans, water vapour, clouds and changes to vegetation. [10]

Warming is bringing other unpredictable changes. Melting glaciers and precipitation are causing some rivers to overflow, while evaporation is emptying others. Diseases are spreading. Some crops grow faster while others see [15]

[(p.97)1]　**conjecture**　推量，推測，憶測．
[(p.97)3]　**permafrost**　(北極地方の)永久凍土層．
[(p.97)3]　**shantytown**　(都市の)ぼろ家地区，貧民街．
[(p.97)5]　**heat wave**　(長い)酷暑，熱波．
[(p.97)11]　**solar cycle**　太陽周期．太陽の黒点数が変化する周期．ほぼ 11 年．太陽活動の他のすべての現象も，この周期にしたがっている．
[(p.97)12]　**climatologist**　気候学士，風土学士．climatology は「気候学，風土学」．
[(p.97)13]　**IPCC (= Intergovernmental Panel on Climate Change)**　気候変動に関する政府間パネル．世界気象機関（WMO）傘下．1988 年に初会合．
[1]　**tonne (= ton)**　トン．
[5]　**greenhouse gas**　温室効果ガス．温室効果を引き起こす気体．特に二酸化炭素，フロンなど．
[5]　**trap**　この場合は，「(気体・エネルギーなどを)のがさないようにする，封じ込める」．
[6]　**troposphere**　対流圏(地表から約 10–20 km の間)．
[7]　**methane**　メタン．無味無臭無色の気体．天然ガスの主成分．
[7]　**chlorofluorocarbon**　クロロフルオロカーボン．塩素化・フッ素化されたメタンやエタンの総称．慣用名フロン．冷媒・噴霧剤・発泡剤に使われるが，オゾン層を破壊することから生産禁止に向かっている．略 CFC．
[8]　**cosmic ray**　宇宙線．(通例複数形で用いられる．)
[9]　**atmospheric**　大気(中)の，空気の．
[15]　**precipitation**　降雨[雪]，降水．

yields slashed by disease and drought. Clashes over dwindling water resources may cause conflicts in many regions.

As natural ecosystems — such as coral reefs — are disrupted, biodiversity is reduced. Most species cannot migrate fast enough to keep up, though others are already evolving in response to warming.

Thermal expansion of the oceans, combined with melting ice on land, is also raising sea levels. In this century, human activity could trigger an irreversible melting of the Greenland ice sheet. This would condemn the world to a rise in sea level of six metres — enough to flood land occupied by billions of people.

The global warming would be more pronounced if it were not for sulphur particles and other pollutants that shade us, and because forests and oceans absorb around half of the CO_2 we produce. But the accumulation rate of atmospheric CO_2 has doubled since 2001, suggesting that nature's ability to absorb the gas could now be stretched to the limit. Recent research suggests that natural CO_2 "sinks", like peat bogs and forests, are actually starting to release CO_2.

Deeper cuts

At the Earth Summit in 1992, the world agreed to prevent "dangerous"

---

[3]   **ecosystem** 生態系.
[3]   **coral reef** さんご礁.
[3]   **biodiversity** 生物(の)多様性.
[7, 8, 10]   **could, would** 7行目の could, 8行目と10行目の would は,「〜してしまうかもしれない」「〜してしまうだろう」というように仮定の意味で使われる助動詞である. could や would であるからといって, 決して過去のことを言っているわけではないので, 注意. この would や could の用法については, 拙者『新ほんとうの英語がわかる ネイティヴに「こころ」を伝えたい』(新潮選書)の173から181ページで解説した.
[8]   **ice sheet** 氷床. 南極大陸や Greenland で見られる広い範囲をおおう氷河.
[10]   **sulphur** 硫黄(いおう). sulfur とも書く.
[11]   **particle** (微)分子, 粒子; 小片; 素粒子.
[15]   **sink** この場合は, 動詞としてではなく, 名詞として使われていて,「シンク, 沈む場所」.
[15]   **peat bog** 泥炭湿地[湿原], 泥炭地.
[19]   **the Earth summit in 1992** 1992年にブラジル・リオデジャネイロで開かれたリオ地球サミットのこと. THE WORLD TODAY の"The summit that couldn't save itself" も参照のこと.

SCIENCE AND TECHNOLOGY

climate change. The first step was the 1997 Kyoto Protocol, which will now finally come into force during 2005. It will bring modest emission reductions from industrialised countries. But many observers say deeper cuts are needed and developing nations, which have large and growing populations, will one day have to join in. [5]

Some, including the US Bush administration, say the scientific uncertainty over the pace of climate change is grounds for delaying action. The US and Australia have reneged on Kyoto. But most scientists believe we are underestimating the dangers.

In any case, according to the IPCC, the world needs to quickly improve the [10] efficiency of its energy usage and develop renewable non-carbon fuels like: wind, solar, tidal, wave and perhaps nuclear power. It also means developing new methods of converting this clean energy into motive power, like hydrogen fuel cells for cars.

Other less conventional solutions include ideas to stave off warming by [15] "mega-engineering" the planet with giant mirrors to deflect the Sun's rays, seeding the oceans with iron to generate algal blooms, or burying greenhouse gases below the sea.

The bottom line is that we will need to cut CO_2 emissions by 70% to 80% simply to stabilise atmospheric CO_2 concentrations — and thus temperatures. [20] The quicker we do that, the less unbearably hot our future world will be.

---

[1] **the 1997 Kyoto Protocol** 気候変動に関する国際連合枠組条約の京都議定書 (Kyoto Protocol to the United Nations Framework Convention on Climate Change). 気候変動枠組条約に基づき，1997年に京都市の国立京都国際会館で開かれた地球温暖化防止京都会議 (第3回気候変動枠組条約締約国会議，COP3) で議決した議定書．AMERICA AND THE WORLD の "Hidden power" を参照のこと．

[8] **renege on** （約束などを）破る，（協定などに）背く．renege on one's promise で，「約束を破る」．例 The president promised lower taxes, but he reneged on his promise and raised them instead. （大統領は減税を約束したが，それを破ったばかりか，増税までしたのだ．）

[19] **bottom line** 要点，肝心かなめ．"The bottom line is that you mustn't lose this opportunity." で，「要はこの機会を逃さないことだ」となる．例 The bottom line is that either you know the words on the test or not. （結局 [肝心なのは]，君が試験に出る単語を知ってるかどうかだ．）

[20] **stabilise** 安定させる [する]．特にアメリカ英語では stabilize と綴る．

Climate change

Questions

1. The word "lethal" on page 97, line 4, is closest in meaning to

   (A) deadly
   (B) legal
   (C) illegal
   (D) harmless

2. What does "the degree of warming" as it is used on page 98, line 12, mean?

   (A) the number of degrees the temperature rises
   (B) the amount of concentration of CO2 in the atmosphere
   (C) the content of the atmosphere today compared with pre-industrial levels
   (D) the extent of the rise in temperature

3. The word "dwindling" on page 99, line 1, is closest in meaning to

   (A) increasing
   (B) decreasing
   (C) growing
   (D) exploding

4. What does the author mean by "Clashes over dwindling water resources may cause conflicts in many regions." on page 99, lines 1–2?

   (A) Water levels in many countries will continue to become lower.
   (B) People around the world may fight over water.
   (C) Conflicting ideas may arise as to why water is become more scarce.
   (D) Scientists may begin to argue about how to solve the problem of limited water supplies.

5. The sentence "This would condemn the world to a rise in sea level of six meters." on page 99, lines 8–9, can be rewritten

   (A) This would save the world from a rise in sea level of six meters.
   (B) This would sentence the world to a rise in sea level of six meters.
   (C) This would satisfy the world with a rise in sea level of six meters.
   (D) This would deliver the world from a rise in sea level of six meters.

SCIENCE AND TECHNOLOGY

6. What does "more pronounced" on page 99, line 10, mean?

(A) worse
(B) more talked about
(C) less in evidence
(D) more silent in its effect

7. According to the author, Pres. Bush seems to believe that

(A) most scientists underestimate the danger and this is grounds for delaying action
(B) climate change is grounds for delaying action on the Kyoto Protocol
(C) we don't need to move now on climate change because scientists can't agree on its pace
(D) reneging on the Kyoto Protocol will only lead to further delaying action on climate change

8. Name two countries that have refused to sign the Kyoto Protocol?

(A) the U.S. and Japan
(B) Japan and Australia
(C) the U.S. and Australia
(D) the U.S. and China

You will hear the entire text of "Climate change: instant expert." Immediately following the text, you will hear Questions 9 and 10.
Listen carefully to the text and questions, and write your answers in the space provided below.

9. _____

10. _____

Great telescope race

Nigel Henbest

introduction

　この記事を書いた Nigel Henbest は、イギリスを中心に活躍する、よく知られた天文学関係のライター / コメンテーターである。ヘンベストは、2004 年 10 月 20 日付けの *The Independent* 紙に寄稿したこの記事で、世界および宇宙で開発中の最新天体望遠鏡について紹介している。

　工学技術の進歩によって、望遠鏡の集光力 (light-gathering power) は日々向上している。膨張をつづける宇宙においては、当然のことであるが、遠くの世界が見られれば見られるほど、そこで起こった出来事もそれに合わせてもっと昔にさかのぼって確認できる。何十億光年も離れた星の様子を確認できれば、そこで何十億年も前に起こったこともわかるかもしれない。宇宙が生まれたその瞬間をこの目で確認できる日が来るのも、あるいはそれほど遠くないかもしれない。

　平和な国際協力を考える上で、天文観測以上にすばらしいものがほかにあるだろうか？　宇宙の遠くかなたからこちらを眺めれば、われわれはみな「太陽系第三惑星」と呼ばれる岩石の上に住んでいる生物に過ぎないのだから。

　　High above the Earth, a gargantuan telescope peers into space. It dwarfs the Hubble Telescope, the twentieth-century's greatest scientific instrument. With a mirror half the size of a tennis court, the Next Generation Space Telescope will reveal the edges of the observable Universe.

　　The Next Generation Space Telescope is already on the drawing board. [5] Within 10 years, this ultimate telescope will be flying in space. Instead of orbiting the Earth, the Next Generation Space Telescope will follow its own orbit around the Sun. But its designers will place it at a special balance point, outside Earth's own orbit. At this location, the so-called Lagrangian-2 point, our planet's gravity still ensnares the telescope, so it travels round the Sun [10] always a million miles from the Earth.

　　Huge solar panels will provide the telescope with power, and — just as important — shield it from the Sun's heat. Cooled down to the temperature of deep space, the Next Generation Space Telescope can observe faint heat signals from the farthest reaches of the Universe. It will peer beyond where even [15] Hubble can see, to the very edges of the observable Universe.

SCIENCE AND TECHNOLOGY

Because light takes billions of years to travel this far, the Next Generation Space Telescope will be seeing these distant regions as they were billions of years ago — just after the Big Bang in which everything began.

This ultimate telescope combines the clear views that Hubble enjoys with the mammoth size of the biggest telescopes currently being built on the ground. [5]

In the dry deserts of Chile, astronomers are this year completing the most powerful telescope ever constructed on Earth. The Very Large Telescope in fact comprises four telescopes, on the peak of a mountain that has been blasted flat to form a platform for the cosmic quartet. Each of the telescopes has a mirror 8 metres (26 feet) across. Linked together, the four instruments will collect as [10] much light as single telescopes over 50 feet in size.

Three of the four telescopes are already working, and astronomers have been astounded by the quality of their views of the cosmos — of glowing nebulae, dying stars and distant galaxies.

To construct such a vast telescope, its builders have pushed engineering to [15] the limit. In particular, the telescope must tilt to turn to different galaxies, giving gravity a purchase on its huge — but thin — mirror. If gravity bends the

---

[(p.103)1] **gargantuan** 巨大な；遠大な，途方もない．

[(p.103)1] **dwarf** 小さくする［見せる］．例 The budget of Japan dwarfs that of Australia. After all, there are about six times as many people in Japan as in Australia.（日本の国家予算に比べると，オーストラリアの国家予算はかすんでしまう．何と言っても，日本の人口は，オーストラリアの人口の6倍だ．）

[(p.103)2] **the Hubble Telescope**（= the Hubble Space Telescope） ハッブル宇宙望遠鏡．NASAの主鏡口径2.4 mの望遠鏡．1990年，スペースシャトルDiscoveryから放出された．

[(p.103)3-4] **the Next Generation Space Telescope** 次世代宇宙望遠鏡．

[(p.103)9] **Lagrangian** ラグランジアン，ラグランジュ関数．

[(p.103)12] **solar panel** 太陽電池板．

[7] **the Very Large Telescope,**（VLT） 超大型［大規模］望遠鏡．

[9] **quartet** 四つ組，四つぞろい．the cosmic quartetは，4本の望遠鏡が集まってでてきているthe Very Large Telescopeのことを指している．

[14] **nebulae** 星雲；銀河．

[17] **giving gravity a purchase on...** 「望遠鏡は別の銀河を観測するためにどちらかに傾く必要があるが，その際に重力が，大きな——しかし薄い——鏡に悪影響を及ぼしてしまう」ということ．purchaseは「手掛かり，足掛かり」，to give a purchase onは「足掛かりを与える」，したがって，この場合は，「望遠鏡が傾いてしまうと，鏡に重力が加わってしまう」ということ．to get purchase on...（...に足掛かり［手掛かり］を得る）のほうがむしろよく使われるかもしれない．例

mirror by an amount smaller than the width of a human hair, the telescope's view of giant galaxies is blurred to uselessness. So the designers have attached the back of the mirror to hundreds of moving supports, computer-controlled to push the mirror back into shape — a millionth of an inch at a time — as the telescope tilts.

While telescopes in Chile are placed to view the southern sky, the best place on Earth for observing the northern heavens is the 14,000-foot high peak of Mauna Kea, Hawaii. Here, astronomers have constructed the world's biggest astronomical observatory. Put together, the total area of the mirrors in these telescopes would outstrip even the Very Large Telescope. But these instruments are competitors, each seeking to be the most powerful telescope observing the northern part of the sky.

Gemini North is the latest, starting work this year. The surface of its mirror is so smooth that if you enlarged it to the size of the Earth, the largest bump would be only a foot high. Next door is the Japanese telescope Subaru, with the biggest single mirror in the world — almost 8.3 metres (27 feet) across. Like the Very Large Telescope, it has hundreds of supports, actively pushing the mirror into the precisely correct shape.

But the jewels in the crown of Mauna Kea are the pair of Keck Telescopes. Each has a mirror 10 metres (33 feet) across. No-one could manufacture a single piece of glass that size, so the Keck mirror is made of 36 pieces, each just six feet across, fitted together like bathroom tiles. A perfect fit between the tiles is ensured by a computer-activated system, pushing on the back of each segment to ensure the tiled mirror forms a single perfectly smooth surface. To spread the forces evenly, the support system is based on a design used to even

---

That block of concrete is so big and smooth, I can't get a purchase on it.（そのコンクリートの塊はあまりにも大きくてなめらかなので，それを持ち上げることができない［どこを持って持ち上げたらいいかわからない］．） 例 The tires slipped on the road and couldn't get a purchase on it.（タイヤは道の上で滑ってしまって，路面をしっかり嚙むことができなかった．）

[8]　**Mauna Kea**　マウナケア．Hawaii 島中北部の死火山．
[10]　**outstrip**　この場合は，「．．．よりまさる，上回る，凌駕する」．
[13]　**Gemini North**　ジェミニ・ノース望遠鏡．
[15]　**the Japanese telecope Subaru**　the Subaru Telescope（すばる望遠鏡）のこと．
[19]　**the Keck Telescope**　ケック望遠鏡．

SCIENCE AND TECHNOLOGY

out the force of horses pulling a Wild West covered wagon!

The first Keck telescope has been observing for eight years, and it has revolutionised astronomy, from discovering tiny ice planets beyond Pluto, to tracking planets of other stars — and pinning down the distances to the farthest known galaxies, over 10 billion light years away. [5]

Texas has an even bigger panelled telescope, the Hobby-Eberly Telescope, some 12 metres (almost 40 feet) in diameter. Its design has brought it in at only one-tenth the cost of Keck, with the payoff that it cannot focus quite as accurately. Its strength, instead, will come from splitting up the light from distant objects in more detail than any other telescope. [10]

On Mount Graham, in Arizona, the world's 'biggest binoculars' are about to peer at the sky. The Large Binocular Telescope has two giant mirrors — each 8.4 metres (27 feet) across — mounted on the same frame. But astronomers here have decided against the complication of using hundreds of computer-controlled supports to keep the mirror in shape. [15]

Instead, they have made the world's biggest glass honeycomb, with its front curved to focus starlight. The empty honeycomb structure behind keeps the mirror rigid enough to stay in shape as the telescope tilts, without complicated support structures. At the same time, it is much lighter in weight than a solid mirror of the same proportions. [20]

These 'ten-metre' class telescopes are giving the Hubble Space Telescope a good run for its money. Although Hubble has the sharpest views of the distant Universe, it is puny compared to these giants: its mirror is outranked by some 30 telescopes on the ground. Each of the huge Keck Telescopes in Hawaii, for example, collects so much light that it can "see" stars 10 times fainter than [25]

[(p.105)25–1] **even out** ここでは，「（負担など）均等[公平]にする」．したがって，このセンテンスは，「36枚の鏡を押す力を均等に広げるために，その制御システムは西部の幌馬車を引く馬の脚力にも相当する力が出せるように設計されている」ということ．

[3] **Pluto** 冥王星(めいおうせい)．

[6] **the Hobby-Eberly Telescope** HET 望遠鏡

[12] **the Large Binocular Telescope** (LBT) 大型双眼望遠鏡

[16] **glass honeycomb** これは the Large Binocular Telescope の二つの鏡の背後に付けられた重量700トン，高さ52mの箱型キューポラ(溶銑(ようせん)炉)のこと．

Hubble can perceive. Astronomers routinely search out strange distant galaxies with Hubble's sharp eye, then analyse their light with the vast collecting power of Keck.

 The Next Generation Space Telescope will combine Hubble's sharp views with the power of today's large telescopes on Earth. And so, some astronomers are moving on to dream up even bigger instruments that could be built on terra firma. The most audacious plan of all is the OverWhelmingly Large Telescope.

The OverWhelmingly Large Telescope — OWL for short — would have a mirror 100 metres across. That is as big as a radio telescope like Jodrell Bank or the Green Bank radio dish in West Virginia. In everyday terms, we are thinking not so much of a tennis court but of a football pitch.

The OWL concept has been hatched by astronomers from the European Southern Observatory, which has built the Very Large Telescope in Chile. Inspired by the segmented mirrors of Keck and the Hobby-Eberly telescope in Texas, they propose fitting together some 1600 separate hexagonal mirrors, to create a mirror surface 100 metres across. It will be housed in a vast metal framework that can swivel to point to any part of the sky.

If OWL is built, it will have the power to pick out individual stars in galaxies halfway across the Universe, and to see planets in orbit around other stars. It may take us on the final step to answering the ultimate questions about the beginning and end of the Universe, and the existence of life elsewhere.

[6–7] **terra firma** 乾いた[堅い]土地，大地，陸地．
[7] **the OverWhelmingly Large Telescope (OWL)** 圧倒的大型望遠鏡．OverWhelming と Over-whelming の W が大文字で表記されている．1990 年代から，会社名や商品名にこういう書き方がよく見られるようになった．商品名の iPod や iMac，検索エンジンの AltaVista などもそうだ．OverWhelmingly と書くと，意味が変わるわけではもちろんないが，なんとなくカッコいい感じになる．
[9] **radio telescope** 電波望遠鏡．天体からの電波を観測するためのアンテナ．
[9] **Jodrell Bank** ジョドレルバンク．イギリス北西部チェシャー州北東部のマックルズフィールド (Macclesfield) にある Manchester University の天文台．
[10] **Green Bank radio dish** アメリカのウェストヴァージニア州グリーンバンクにある巨大な電波望遠鏡 the Green Bank Telescope のこと．アメリカ国立電波天文台が運用している．
[15] **hexagonal** 六角形の，六辺形の．
[19] **halfway** この場合は，「ある程度；かなり」．

SCIENCE AND TECHNOLOGY

Questions

1. A major difference between the Hubble Telescope and the Next Generation Space Telescope is that

   (A) the latter orbits the Sun while the former orbits the Earth
   (B) the former is larger but not as powerful as the latter
   (C) Earth's gravity affects the former but not the latter
   (D) solar panels power the latter but not the former

2. According to the article, the best place on Earth for observing the northern sky is the 14,000-foot-high peak of Mauna Kea, Hawaii. Approximately how many metres is 14,000 feet?

   (A) about 4800 metres
   (B) about 4200 metres
   (C) about 40,020 metres
   (D) about 480 metres

3. The telescopes on Mauna Kea in Hawaii

   (A) are linked together to observe the Universe
   (B) are huge, but not as big as the Very Large Telescope
   (C) compete with telescopes in Chile to observe the northern part of the sky
   (D) try to outdo each other in what they observe

4. What does "pinning down" on page 106, line 4, mean?

   (A) observing
   (B) estimating
   (C) determining
   (D) announcing

5. Who built the Very Large Telescope?

   (A) NASA
   (B) the Green Bank
   (C) the European Southern Observatory
   (D) the National Astronomical Observatory of Japan

6. Which telescope does NOT match the location?

(A) the OverWhelmingly Large Telescope — West Virginia
(B) the Large Binocular Telescope — Arizona
(C) the Hobby-Eberly Telescope — Texas
(D) the Very Large Telescope — Chile

7. Which telescope does NOT match the size of mirror?

(A) the Very Large Telescope — 8.3 metres
(B) the OverWhelmingly Large Telescope — 100 metres
(C) the Keck Telescopes — 10 metres each
(D) the Hobby-Eberly Telescope — 12 metres

8. Why do astronomers want bigger telescopes?

(A) to compete with each other
(B) to rival radio telescopes such as the one at Jodrell Bank
(C) to keep observation here on terra firm
(D) to see farther into space

You will hear the entire text of "Great telescope race." Immediately following the text, you will hear Questions 9 and 10.

Listen carefully to the text and questions, and write your answers in the space provided below.

9. _____

10. _____

FICTION

The art of Saito Makoto

Roger Pulvers

introduction

　この短編は、『時事英語研究』（現在、休刊）の1993年11月号に発表したものである。1983年、ぼくらはイギリスのエセックス州に住む妻の叔母 Isabel Rawsthorne のもとを訪れたが、そのとき叔母からある話を聞かされた。叔母のその話を題材にして、ぼくはこの物語を書いた。

　イザベル叔母は、若い頃は有名な芸術モデルとして活躍していた。ジャコメッティ、ピカソ、ドラン、エプスタインといった画家や彫刻家のためにポーズを取っていたのだ。実際、イザベル叔母はジャコメッティに対しては創作モデルを務めただけでなく、しばらく一緒に暮していた。

　イザベル叔母の話によると、戦前、どうやらジャコメッティを崇拝する若い日本人がいたらしい。その若い日本人はイタリア系スイス人の彫刻家・画家アルベルト・ジャコメッティを心から崇拝していて、ジャコメッティ自身は叔母と付き合っていた頃は大変貧しい暮しをしていたにもかかわらず、自分もその尊敬する人とまったく同じ格好をしなければならない、と考えたようである。ジャコメッティに弟子入りした日本人青年は、そのように師匠を真似ることで、必ずその芸術に近づける、と信じたのだ。

　イザベル叔母にその話を聞いたぼくは、こうして自分の物語のなかに「斎藤誠」という人物を作り上げることができた。

Please allow me to tell you about my husband, Saito Makoto. I hope that you will not think me lacking in devotion for him when you hear his story. It is only now, many years after his death, that I am finally able to understand what happened to him.

　Saito was a most talented painter, a man recognized at an early age for his [5] talent. The famous art critic, Masami Goichi, wrote of Saito . . .

　　His gift is undeniable. He reminds one immediately of Braque, but there are also undertones of playfulness, à la Miro, Kandinsky and Klee.

[10]

　　If there is a problem it is: Who is Saito? He is an artist who will have to find *himself* before he finds his art.

Masami Goichi wrote that in an issue of *Geijutsu Shincho*. Upon reading that Saito ripped all of his copies of the magazine to shreds.

"I know who I am," he hollered, throwing the magazine, like confetti, out our second-storey apartment window. "Let Masami go to hell where he will no doubt find *himself*!"

I had never seen Saito so angry before. He was determined, from that time on, to make a name for himself in the Japanese art world.

We were living then at Futago Tamagawa. Saito used to take long walks along the river, not coming back until dark. He ate and drank, then set out to work throughout the night. I myself was working as a nursery school teacher in Seijo Gakuenmae. Saito was not selling many of his paintings but we were not short of money by any means.

My father had considerable wealth which he was able to hold onto despite the war. My father's father had built a successful business manufacturing bicycle frames. Everyone after the war wanted to own a bicycle and the business went from strength to strength.

My family was very generous toward me and Saito. Father gave us the apartment that we were living in.

"Your husband is a man of genius," he told me. "I am happy if I can help him express that genius, and so should you be."

Father died in a bicycle accident in 1964, the year of the Tokyo Olympics.

Even though Saito had shredded all of his copies of *Geijutsu Shincho*, he was unable to rid Masami Goichi's words from his mind. Then, one day, he read some words written by the Italian sculptor Alberto Giacometti and those words changed his life . . . and mine.

[(p.112)8] **Braque, Georges** (1882–1963)　ブラック．フランスの画家．ピカソとともにキュビズムを発展させる．

[(p.112)9] **à la**　…流の[に]；…式の[に]．a la とも書く．

[(p.112)9] **Miro, Joan** (1893–1983)　ミロ．スペインのシュールレアリスムの画家．

[(p.112)9] **Kandinsky, Wassily** (1866–1944)　カンディンスキー．ロシア生まれの画家．抽象画の創始者の一人．

[(p.112)9] **Klee, Paul** (1879–1940)　クレー．スイスの画家．鮮やかな色彩が特徴．

[16]　**go from strength to strength**　急速に力をつけてくる．どんどんよくなる．

[24]　**Giacometti, Alberto** (1901–66)　ジャコメッティ．イタリア系スイス人の彫刻家・画家．独特の折れそうに細い人物像で知られる．

The terrible thing is: the more one works on a picture, the more impossible it becomes to finish it.

Saito wrote a letter to Giacometti telling him that this was a "very Japanese concept," and that "you have shown me a great truth about the artistic process, something that I have suspected but never grasped until today."

Saito pored over western art magazines, searching for photographs and prints of Giacometti's drawings and sculpture. On a very hot night around Obon he returned from one of his walks along the Tamagawa going straight to his studio without eating or drinking. I heard him mumbling to himself in his studio and slid the door open. He was pacing the floor back and forth. I asked him what the matter was.

He stopped in his tracks and looked at me sternly.

"The matter is that I have been trying to get too close to my subjects and have been losing myself in the details. I must meet Giacometti. I must!"

He started pacing the floor again, refused all food for that day and the next, came down with a case of viral pneumonia and had to be hospitalized for ten days.

While Saito was in the hospital a registered letter arrived from Italy and I rushed to deliver it to him. It was from Alberto Giacometti himself. He wrote . . .

I am a great admirer of the Japanese and have a very good friend in Mr. Isaku Yanaihara, the eminent professor.

If you wish to come to visit me, I would be most pleased.

Upon reading this letter Saito stood up from bed, though he was still consid-

---

[17] **viral** ウイルス(性)の. 発音にも注意 (/váɪərəl/).
[17] **pneumonia** 肺炎.
[19] **registered letter** 書留郵便物.
[22–23] **Yanaihara, Isaku** (1918–89) 矢内原伊作. 東大総長を務めた経済学者, 矢内原忠雄の長男として, 愛媛県に生まれる. 父忠雄の気質を受け継いだ自由主義者として, 幅広い近代ヨーロッパ的教養をもとに, 平易なことばと文章で人生論・芸術論を中心に論じた. ジャコメッティと交流を深め, 彼の絵画や彫像のモデルをたびたび務めた.

erably weak on his feet, and did his own variety of the Awa Odori around the ward. The other patients in the ward, mostly old men, sat up in bed and clapped their hands as Saito danced from one end of the room to the other.

When Saito returned home from the hospital he was a new man. He started to paint his pictures during the day, as Giacometti apparently did.

"The light must be natural," he said. "I have been dishonest in my art up to now, trying to live my life according to a pattern of what the modern Japanese artist deems artistic."

He carried his old paintings and drawings to the bank of the Tamagawa and burnt every last one of them. Then he wrote an open letter to *Geijutsu Shincho* proclaiming that his art up to then was false . . .

I renounce everything that I have done to date. The name Saito Makoto may be written at the bottom of those paintings, but it is not the same Saito Makoto who is writing this letter. That man is dead. Long live the new Saito Makoto!

I was rather happy, actually, to see the new Saito Makoto. Because we were both doing our work in the daytime Saito and I were now able to spend evenings together. Saito loved the theatre, taking me to see the latest plays by Kinoshita Junji and Tanaka Chikao. He was even asked by Kinoshita Junji to do set decoration for an upcoming play. But he was unable to accept. Saito had made up his mind to go to Italy and meet the great master himself, Alberto Giacometti.

We had moved out of our apartment in Futago Tamagawa and my younger sister, newly married, had taken it over. But father had bought us a large house, with ample room for Saito's studio, in Seijo 5-chome. This also brought me closer to the nursery.

---

[11]　**proclaim**　(...を)宣言する; 公布する.
[13]　**renounce**　(...を)(公式に)放棄する, 棄権する; 宣誓して捨てる.
[21]　**Kinoshita, Junji** (1914–)　木下順二. 劇作家. 代表作『夕鶴』.
[21]　**Tanaka, Chikao** (1905–95)　田中千禾夫. 劇作家. 代表作『雲の涯』.

FICTION

When I told father that Saito wished to go to Italy to study art with a great master, father was overjoyed. He gave us 3,000,000 yen, which was an enormous sum of money in those days.

"Tell Saito-san to take the money to Europe. It is a wonderful thing that he is doing. I suppose I wish that I could have become an artist, too. But more people in Japan then needed bicycle frames than picture frames. Now art and culture is what we need. Good luck to him!" [5]

I went to Mitsukoshi on the Ginza and bought Saito the clothes he would need for Europe: six suits tailor-made for him from English wool; neckties and ascot ties from England and France; American shoes; and a heavy Russian [10] sable overcoat for the European winter.

I remember the day so vividly that I saw Saito off at the wharf in Yokohama. He stood high above me on the deck, wrapped in his black overcoat. To either side of him were elderly European or American people, I cannot tell the difference. But no one was waving from the deck, not the elderly white people [15] and not Saito.

I did not see my husband for more than two years. On the day of his return I put on my very best kimono, one given to me by my grandmother. Father insisted that I travel from Seijo to the wharf at Yokohama in his company [20] limousine. Saito had not written often to me and though we had been married for three years before his departure, I somehow felt that I was travelling in that limousine to meet a half-stranger.

I waited outside the customs area for several hours. It was a bitterly cold late December day and I was happy that I had bought him that heavy fur overcoat. [25] What Saito needed now was some good, warm Japanese home cooking. I had awakened at the crack of dawn that day and prepared his favorite food for him, *niku jaga*.

I must admit to having suffered a shock that morning. Emerging from the customs area was my husband . . . but I cannot say that I immediately recog- [30] nized him.

He was gaunt nearly to the point of emaciation. His chin and cheeks were

---

[32]　**gaunt**　やせた，やせ衰えた．

covered in a straggly greyish beard; and his skimpy clothes were, in a word, rags. He wore a red and white bandana around his neck and on his head an olive green beret with a hole in the side.

Saito was suffering from pleurisy. The driver of the limousine drove us directly to the hospital, but Saito's pneumonia returned and he passed away a week to the day after setting foot in Japan. [5]

What I came to realize years later was that he had met Alberto Giacometti and believed that to create art like him he had to look like him and live his style of life.

In that sense the art critic Masami Goichi was right. But Saito did find himself in Italy. The terrible thing was: he lost his art in the process. [10]

When we scattered Saito's ashes over Tokyo Bay [which was his last wish] I could not help but recall the tiny shreds of paper that he himself had flung out of our old second-storey apartment window by the river at Futago Tamagawa.

[(p.116)32]　**emaciation**　やつれ，憔悴(しょうすい).
[1]　**straggly**　不規則に伸びた.
[1]　**greyish**（= grayish）　灰色[ねずみ色]がかった.
[4]　**pleurisy**　胸膜炎.

ロジャー・パルバース（Roger Pulvers）

1944年ニューヨーク生まれ。作家、劇作家、演出家。UCLAおよびハーバード大学大学院で学ぶ。ワルシャワ、パリに留学ののち、67年に初来日。著書に『ほんとうの英語がわかる　51の処方箋』『新ほんとうの英語がわかる　ネイティヴに「こころ」を伝えたい』『ほんとうの英会話がわかる　ストーリーで学ぶ口語表現』（ともに新潮選書）、『キュート・デビルの魔法の英語　The Cute Devil and the Twelve Lands』『五行でわかる日本文学　英日狂演滑稽五行詩　There was an Old Pond with a Frog and other literary limericks』（ともに研究社）、『旅する帽子　小説ラフカディオ・ハーン』『ライス』（ともに講談社）、『日本ひとめぼれ』（岩波同時代ライブラリー）など、訳書に井上ひさし『父と暮せば　英文対訳』（こまつ座）、宮沢賢治『英語で読む　銀河鉄道の夜』、坂口安吾『英語で読む　桜の森の満開の下』（ともにちくま文庫）などがある。現在、東京工業大学教授。

　ホームページは、Roger Pulvers Official Site(http://www17.ocn.ne.jp/~h-uesugi/).

SETTING THE STAGE（セッティング・ザ・ステージ）
——Articles and Essays about the State of Our World Today——

2005年10月31日　初版発行
2009年9月30日　5刷発行

編著者●ロジャー・パルバース
Edited and with Commentary by Roger Pulvers

Copyright © 2005 by Roger Pulvers

発行者●関戸雅男

発行所●株式会社　研究社
〒102-8152　東京都千代田区富士見2-11-3
電話　編集(03)3288-7711(代)　営業(03)3288-7777(代)
振替　00150-9-26710
http://www.kenkyusha.co.jp/

KENKYUSHA
〈検印省略〉

印刷所●研究社印刷株式会社

装丁●久保和正

本文デザイン●古正佳緒里

編集協力●鹿児島有里

ISBN978-4-327-42167-0　C1082　Printed in Japan

本書の無断複写(コピー)は著作権法上での例外を除き、禁じられています。
落丁本、乱丁本はお取り替え致します。
価格はカバーに表示してあります。

ロジャー・パルバース 著 上杉隼人 訳

夏休みの
リーディング
学習に
最適!

キュート・デビルの魔法の英語
The Cute Devil and the Twelve Lands

ぼくは英語学習の救世主だ。この本を読めば、日本人のわずらわしい英語学習地獄から抜け出して、英語を自由に使いこなせる国に行けるよ。本書を最後まで読み終えたみなさんは、きっと魔法の英語力が身についているはずさ。

ほんとうさ、キュート・デビルは絶対に嘘をつかないよ。はっはっは、ひっひっひ、ほっほっほ！(Believe me, the Cute Devil never lies. Ha ha ha hee hee hee ho ho ho!)

愉快な12の短篇小説を英語で楽しんで(全篇対訳つき)、さらにネイティヴスピーカーの英語表現もしっかり学べる、画期的な英語学習書！

読者のみなさんが、著者ロジャー・パルバース(労蛇)とともに訪れる12のあの世の世界(Other Worlds)は……
そしてキュート・デビルは、そこでいつもあなたを待っています……

The Land of Pulp （パルプの国）出版界の地獄
The Land of Inchiki （インチキの国）証券・金融界の地獄
The Land of Negate （何に対してもケチをつける国）批評家・評論家の地獄
The Land of Recycle （リサイクルの国）コンピュータの地獄
The Land of Absolute （絶対なるものの国）宗教界の地獄
The Land of Hospitalia （ホスピタリアの国）医療界の地獄
The Land of Hyperbia （超でっち上げの国）広告業界の地獄
The Land of R.I.P.-Off （ぼろ儲けの国）不動産業界の地獄
The Land of Verisimilia （真実らしさの国）マスコミ業界の地獄
The Land of Litigatia （訴訟の国）裁判人・弁護士の地獄
The Land of Celebria （有名人の国）有名人の地獄
The Land of Oblivia （忘却の国）そしてここは、あなたの地獄？

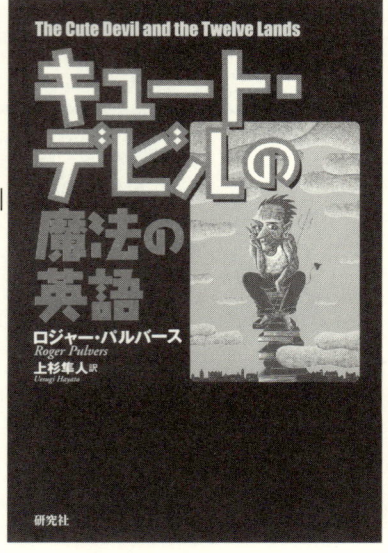

愉快なイラスト満載！
画・磯 良一

ISBN 4-327-45174-6 C1082
定価1,470円（本体1,400円＋税）
四六判 並製 244頁

ロジャー・パルバース 著／柴田元幸 訳／喜多村紀 画

五行でわかる日本文学
英日狂演滑稽五行詩(リメリック)
There was an Old Pond with a Frog and other literary limericks

愛ある冗談(たわごと)
敬意ある揶揄(からかい)
五行詩×25で
日本文学がすっかりわか(らなくな)る！
英／日 笑える詩の狂演

日本文学利目律句(リメリック)
英（ロジャー・パルバース）
日（柴田元幸）狂演滑稽五行詩！

ISBN 4-327-38509-3 C1080
定価1,365円（本体1,300円＋税）
四六判 上製 86頁

価格表示は2008年10月現在のものです。